D1389843

POWERS OF A GIRL

65 MARVEL WOMEN WHO CHANGED THE UNIVERSE

WRITTEN BY Lorraine Cink

ILLUSTRATED BY Alice X. Zhang

LOS ANGELES • NEW YORK

For you.
You have everything you will ever need
already inside of you. You are a universe.

–Lorraine Cink

For my parents.
Thank you for your support since my childhood.

For anyone giving this book to a child.
Thank you for being someone's real-life hero.

–Alice X. Zhang

First published in 2019 by Marvel Press
This edition first published in 2019 by Studio Press Books,
an imprint of Bonnier Books UK,
The Plaza, 535 King's Road, London, SW10 0SZ
www.studiopressbooks.co.uk
www.bonnierbooks.co.uk

© 2019 MARVEL

1 3 5 7 9 10 8 6 4 2

ISBN 978-1-78741-555-3

Written by Lorraine Cink
Illustrated by Alice X. Zhang
Designed by Elizabeth H. Clark and Scott Petrower

Printed in China

TABLE OF CONTENTS

LIONHEARTED LADIES.
GALACTIC GALS.
DARING DAMES.
BAD BAES.

THIS IS THE MARVEL UNIVERSE. Where the personalities, powers, and straight-up legends of countless heroic women have captivated readers for generations. Whether they consider their supernatural abilities a blessing or a curse, these women have gifts as diverse as these heroic ladies themselves. From the powerful punches of America Chavez to the godly zeal of Valkyrie, there's an entire universe of women here to teach us how we all have the power within ourselves to be extraordinary.

I love punch AND punching!

Even as extraordinary as Squirrel Girl. Perhaps the most powerful hero in the entire Marvel Universe, Squirrel Girl has defeated villains as omnipotent as Thanos and as titanic as the city-crushing monstrosity Fin Fang Foom. Although the name Squirrel Girl may not immediately evoke fear, Doreen Green has a surprisingly formidable set of gifts. She is said to have all the powers of a squirrel and all the powers of a girl.

Ooooo, did she just say the name of the book?

Stop breaking the fourth wall, Gwenpool. We haven't gotten to you yet. But I can't wait!

GWEN! Okay, okay. Sheesh!

Sorry about that. Now, where was I? Oh, yeah!

Before Gwenpool interrupts again, I should mention that I'm Lorraine. I live in New York City, the home of Super Heroes. I can almost see Avengers Mansion* from my office window! Well . . . kinda. There's a building in the way.

Since I was a girl, Super Heroes have been a big part of my life, and now I get to talk about them every day as part of my work. I live and breathe this stuff on the daily! I know, right?! But, I've always wished a book existed not just celebrating heroic women in the Marvel Universe, but sharing their struggles, victories, and the lessons we can learn from these laudable ladies. These girls and women can teach us so much more than how to punch hard (though I am HERE for that, too). They can teach us about growth, passion, our innermost selves, and how to become our own heroes.

So what exactly are the powers of a girl? Whether you were born a girl, identify as a girl, or just appreciate how darn cool girls and former girls (or as you might call them: women) just so happen to be, we know that being a girl can bring you great and unforetold powers. And as Spider-Man's Uncle Ben once said, with great power comes great—Eh, you know the rest.

That reminds me . . . from time to time, I might mention boys, or even men, or sometimes boys who put "man" in their name to sound cool. Boys and men are welcome here, too. Everyone is welcome. Hey, we're all in it together, right? Well, except for maybe the Super Villains. Hopefully, if any Super Villains are reading this, they will learn to turn over a new leaf and stop being Grade-A jerks. Anyway, while this book will focus on girls and former girls, everybody is welcome to the girl party because a party alone is . . . well,

* Avengers Mansion is based on a real building in NYC, a museum called the Frick House. Which is pretty frickin' awesome.

awkward. Even the most powerful Super Hero is stronger with the help of her allies. So, join me and other True Believers who dare to seek the wisdom of Marvel Super Hero Girls.

As I was saying, girls have many powers, which we'll explore in this book. And while, yes, some of these girls can fly, punch hard, embiggen, talk to squirrels, and occasionally emit dangerous sparkles, that is far from what makes them super. Super Heroes come in all shapes, sizes, races, religions, genders, sexualities, outfits, and musical tastes, but there is one thing that they all share.

GWEN. NO. Anyways, this brings us to:

An unbridled bloodlust?!

GIRLS:
THE ORIGIN STORY

No Super Hero is born a champion. Even if you just so happen to tumble out of the womb flying, punching hard, embiggening, talking to squirrels, or emitting danger sparkles, the path to heroism requires a choice. The choice to use your powers for good. That's why none of these stories really start at birth. They begin when *something* awful, amazing, clandestine, or all of the above happens. What these girls choose to do with that *something* is what makes them great. Heck, some of these ladies were heroes before they were even super.

Life is full of these choices, and that is where our heroes begin. Girls have choices to do the right thing, and that is their first super-power. SPOILER ALERT: When they start out, some girls may even work with some pretty reprehensible people doing some pretty not-cool things and end up becoming heroes, like Black Widow and Gamora. Sorry to call you out, ladies, but . . . you know what you did.

Here are attributes of a girl that, as we'll see, will make super people become Super Heroes.

#BOOM

I'm such an artist!

That's me!

!WARNING! FLAWS

I just want to get this out in the open now: This isn't going to be one of those books where all the heroes do everything right all the time. In fact, sometimes these girls mess up. Big-time. Sometimes they mess up and bad things happen to them and to the people they love. Sometimes bad things happen and it's not even their fault and they still have to deal with the fallout. No girl is perfect, no matter how super. A lot more can be learned from failures than from always winning, so appreciate these failures! Learning from mistakes and moving on is one heck of a super-power.

SACRIFICES AND HARD WORK

Sometimes doing what is right means giving up other things. Spider-Gwen would much rather hang out with her ax-grinding bandmates, the Mary Janes, than save NYC from the Lizard, but you know, not everything can be rock-star jam sessions. Super-powers won't do all the work for you.

RESPONSIBILITY

It's not just for Spider-Men anymore. Girls can take responsibility for their actions and their communities. A hero sees the world she lives in and knows she can use her powers to improve it. It's her responsibility to make her world better if she can. When Quake sees that the world is being overtaken by evil, instead of submitting, she leads a team of elite forces to save the day. Responsibility also means taking responsibility for her own actions; even Captain Marvel has made some *major* mistakes that meant a *major* (. . . military humor) apology to her bestie,

Spider-Woman. Perhaps this is a harder kind of responsibility because there is no glory, but it doesn't make it any less brave.

EMPATHY

Acknowledging the suffering and needs of others is the first signal to any hero that she must dive into action. These girls see their fellow humans, aliens, and sometimes whole planets, and feel their pain, outrage, and fear. Only then will they truly know how to spring into action and save the day. When Captain Marvel sees the aliens displaced by Thanos, she knows she cannot return to Earth until they have homes because she knows how it must feel to have nowhere to go. This also means she must have empathy for herself, which can be a boatload harder at times. This is why bubble baths were invented.*

TEAM-UPS

Asking for help when you need it is definitely a super-power. Girls know that a super-squad gets it done way faster than going it alone, and that sometimes a job takes more than one lady. Whether it's having equally super backup like BFFs Captain Marvel and Spider-Woman, or having a whole crew of confident baes like She-Hulk, or the HERoes of A-Force, girls get the job done—together.

USING HER SMARTS

Girls use their minds. Take fifteen-year-old Riri Williams, who created her own Iron Man suit in her dorm room at MIT. Or Nadia Van Dyne, the second-generation Wasp who started her own lab of girl geniuses

after deciding that lady scientists weren't getting enough attention. Even the greatest super-genius invests in her mind with education, reading, exploring, getting messy, and stoking the flames of her curiosities. At only nine years old, Lunella Lafayette is the smartest character in the entire Marvel Universe, but she still has a lot to learn.

BEING BRAVE

Girls do brave things! Being brave can mean everything from standing up for what one believes in to simply saying no to something one doesn't want to do. Honestly, the latter is often harder than the former. But don't be mistaken. Being brave doesn't mean she always feels impervious or is never scared. In fact, what makes her so brave is that she keeps going when she feels the most afraid. Ms. Marvel was petrified that she'd disappoint her family by taking on her Super Hero persona—not to mention putting herself in personal peril—but she knew she had to do what was right to protect the lives of her fellow New Jersey teens.

Okay, are you ready? These girls are going to do some awesome things. They're going to beat up baddies, break through to other dimensions, and save the fricking universe!

Obvi!

XO,

Lorraine Cink

And me, Gwenpool!

---

* Not really, but they *are* straight-up magic.

#PREACH

"Have you ever seen a little girl RUN SO FAST she falls down? There's an instant, a fraction of a second before the world catches hold of her again . . . A moment when she's outrun every doubt and fear she's ever had about herself and SHE FLIES.

In that one moment, every little girl
flies. I need to find that again. Like
taking a car out into the desert to see
how fast it can go, I need to find the
E D G E   O F   M E …
And maybe, if I fly far enough,
I'll be able to turn around
and look at the world …
And see where I belong."

— CAROL DANVERS,
CAPTAIN MARVEL

CAPTAIN MARVEL

ACE PILOT. SPARKLEFISTS. LADY BOSS.

CAROL DANVERS grew up in a Boston military family with her parents and two brothers. Although it was a steep uphill battle in her time, Carol *needed* to fly. So she joined the Air Force as soon as she turned eighteen (despite the protests of her father, who believed women weren't as capable as men), taking inspiration from women like aviation hero **HELEN COBB**. It can be very hard to push past the limits others place on you, but Carol knew she must follow her own dreams. She pushed herself to become a top-of-her-class fly girl. Before long, she was bravely piloting an elite Stark plane through enemy territory under the code name "Cheeseburger"—delicious *and* deadly. Carol retired from the Air Force as a colonel, and became the head of security for **NASA**. Oh, did I not yet mention Carol is a straight-up boss? Yeah! She was breaking down barriers long before she got super-powers, silencing anyone who doubted that women were capable of incredible things.

At NASA, Carol met **CAPTAIN MAR-VELL**, a Kree alien who was also a Super Hero on the side. I know what you're thinking. *Wait, isn't Mar-Vell a lot like Marvel?* Well, yes! And for good reason. Carol developed her powers when she was caught in a conflict between Captain Mar-Vell, his foe Yon-Rogg, and a large alien machine called a Psyche-Magnitron. (Listen, these aliens live for hyphens between syllables, so just go with it.) During their alien skirmish, Carol absorbed a great deal of radiation that unlocked **KREE POWERS** within her body. However, they lay dormant until months later—more on that soon.

After aiding Captain Mar-Vell, who was under government investigation, Carol Danvers's career at NASA quickly deteriorated. I mean, she saved the world but pissed off the government. Classic Super Hero mistake. While everything was falling apart, Carol reawakened her passion for writing and began working for *Woman* magazine, owned by the *Daily Bugle*. There she became BFFs with Mary Jane Watson (ya know, Spider-Man's on-again-off-again bae) and enjoyed a normal life until she began having strange blackouts. During these blackouts, new super-powers emerged and transformed her into the Super Hero **MS. MARVEL**. Yeah, that's right. MS. Marvel. And thus, Princess Sparklefists was born! Carol eventually mastered her gifts and began aiding Super Hero teams on the reg. She eventually joined **THE AVENGERS** as one of their major players. In her early days (and later days, for that matter) she had A LOT of drama. The Avengers and Carol have always been on-again, off-again, so let's just say sometimes she was seeing other Super Hero teams.

Name: Carol Danvers

Alias: Captain Marvel

Super-powers: Flight; energy absorption and photon blasts that make her hands sparkle; super-strength; speed; stamina; durability

Nicknames: Ace, Princess Sparklefists

Skills: Ace pilot
Master combatant
Espionage / super-spy
Multilingual, including alien languages such as Kree and Shi'ar
Talented writer

Super Bestie: Jessica Drew, aka Spider-Woman

Club House: Avengers Mansion

Solo Pad: The crown of the Statue of Liberty

Snark Level: 10 out of 10 Tony Snarks

Main Squeeze: War Machine, aka James "Rhodey" Rhodes—(at one point he died in her arms and she didn't handle that very well)

Animal Companion: Chewie—looks like a lovable ginger house cat but is actually a Flerken.*

On a space mission with some "off-again" Super Hero allies, Carol began to channel the powers of a white hole, which transformed her into the ultra-powerful and flame-covered entity **BINARY**. As Binary, her cosmic powers were nearly limitless. Feeling detached from her home planet, she traveled the stars, often teaming up with a very bohemian band of space travelers called the Starjammers and just chilling out across the galaxy.

Over time, the white hole Binary drew her power from began to collapse. Carol returned to Earth to join forces with the rest of its mightiest heroes, the Avengers. After spending some time recuperating with the old Avengers gang, she took on the code name **WARBIRD**, in memory of one of her favorite fighter jets. As Warbird, she was not taking any crap. She was back for vengeance, taking down every villain and criminal around.

The Avengers would need Carol's help once again during the world-altering mental breakdown of the powerful Scarlet Witch, where she turned reality inside out. Carol, seeing her true power in this altered reality, rediscovered her past reality, reclaiming her name as

Ms. Marvel. As you can imagine, all of this name-changing had her ready to take a little solo time.

Carol had always been a military girl, so when Tony Stark needed to enforce the Super Hero Registration Act, Ms. Marvel was ready to lend her muscle to the fight. All super-powered people were forced to register with the government, which created a civil war between Super Heroes. Her best friends were torn apart and fighting—anyone who has lived through high school knows how that goes.

In the wake of all of these global upsets, a new and super-not-cool power arose: Norman Osborn (as in the Green Goblin—yeah, *that* Norman Osborn). Well, he tried to convince Ms. Marvel to join his Dark Avengers, but she refused, because she knows a jerk when she sees one. Instead she joined the **NEW AVENGERS** to stop Osborn's evil agenda and protect the world in secret alongside Captain America, the biggest teddy bear in the good ole U-S-of-A. With only slightly world-ending consequences, Osborn was defeated and the Super Hero Registration Act was repealed. Phew! Ms. Marvel had finally found her home again with Earth's Mightiest Heroes. I mean, what's a world takeover every now and then anyway, right?

BUT WHEN DID CAROL GET PANTS?!

Finally, courtesy of Tony Stark, Carol Danvers was given a fancy new flight suit (**WITH PANTS**, because fighting bad guys is hard enough without your butt showing). Captain America suggested that Carol had earned a new title to go with her new look: **CAPTAIN MARVEL**.

Carol had to do some soul-searching. Mourning the death of her aviation hero and mentor, Helen Cobb, Carol realized that without women like Helen who paved the way, sometimes having to fight her own superiors to prove her worth, Carol might never have gotten to fly in a plane, much less in her new **SUPER HERO FLIGHT SUIT**.

Driven by her admiration for Helen and her father—who she wanted to impress and prove wrong in equal

* An alien creature resembling a cat, but containing pocket dimensions holding a seemingly endless protrusion of tentacles, toothy maws, and eggs to be laid. Very snuggly.

WHY IT MATTERS THAT CAROL DANVERS WAS MS. MARVEL BEFORE SHE WAS CAPTAIN MARVEL

Carol took on the code name Ms. Marvel when she became a Super Hero because of her creation during the Women's Liberation Movement. During this time, honorifics for women were either Miss (if unmarried) or Mrs. (if partnered). However, you will notice men are noted as Mr. whether or not they are married, meaning maybe their status isn't greater or less depending on if they locked it down or not. Around the same time Carol Danvers showed up in comics, the title *Ms.* began to be adopted as an honorific for women in hopes of giving them equal opportunity to that of men, regardless of marital status. When Ms. Marvel was given her name, it meant she wasn't there to be married or to be single—she was there to kick some butts and save some days.

measure—Carol forged her own path to greatness. But sometimes the hardest part of achieving great things is pushing past the limits you put on yourself, even if you are decades deep in super-heroing. So for Helen, for her father, for the long-passed Mar-Vell, for the future of girls and women to follow in her flight path, and yes, for herself, Carol Danvers claimed the name Captain Marvel, a symbol of greatness. Just as Helen paved the road for Carol, Carol must now make way and support future women Super Heroes.

And that's just what she has done. Captain Marvel has saved the world countless times, traveled the cosmos with her cat, **CHEWIE** (who might just be the cutest and creepiest alien in the universe), and spent tons of time hanging with her bestie, Spider-Woman. Now she focuses on protecting the Earth and other planets across the galaxy. Not a bad gig, really.

So Let's Review!

- **US Air Force** (The Cheeseburger years)
- **NASA** (Head of Security, aka Boss Lady)
- **Ms. Marvel** (If ya nasty)
- **Ms. Marvel 2.0** (Struck by lightning)
- **Binary** (2 Hot 2 Handle)
-  **Warbird** (Give them the bird!)
-  **Captain Marvel** (KWEEN)

AMERICA CHAVEZ

POWER PUNCHER. RISING STAR. DREAMER.

BIEN, MI FAMILIA! First off, you need to know that **AMERICA CHAVEZ** likes to punch hard. Not only is she good at it, she has a no-BS policy of punch first and ask questions later when it comes to villains. She is notorious for her sassy mouth, bangin' style, and a smirk that puts Tony Stark to shame. But don't get me wrong—just because America is a *cool* girl doesn't mean she is a *mean* girl. When it comes to friendship, America is THERE for it. We'd all be lucky to have or *be* a friend as supportive as America. Oh! You probably should also know that she hails from a dimension made up exclusively of women called Utopia, but trust me, she is all-American.

America Chavez's story begins on **PLANETA FUERTONA** (part of Utopia so, you know, all women here, too), a world that was invaded by insectoid parasites called La Legion. Super-gross. Think giant evil roaches. Nooo thanks! The gods that created Planeta Fuertona sent an ice age over the planet to cleanse it of the invaders. America's grandmother Madrimar punched a star portal (pretty tough abuela) through to the **UTOPIAN PARALLEL**, an alternate dimension. There the women of Fuertona could be safe and wait for their planet to heal, and, ya know, not freeze their cookies off.

America's mothers, Amalia and Elena, met and fell in love in this alternate dimension. On the day of America's birth, Madrimar left the Utopian Parallel to go back to rebuild Planeta Fuertona. America had a relatively normal and happy existence as a tiny girl who gained super-powers from absorbing the **DEMIURGE**. What's the Demiurge, you ask? Just a sentient life force that seeded the planets and created the elder gods. Stay with me, people. America and her family of literal strong-women were imbued with power punches, interdimensional travel through star portals, and of course, flight through those perfectly punched star portals. Can you imagine having so many super-powered ladies to look up to?! Sure, you can! They're everywhere, even if our dimension tends to have ladies with different kinds of powers.

When America was only six years old, black holes threatened to engulf her home in the Utopian Parallel. To save their people, America's mothers sacrificed themselves to heal the rift that threatened their dimension. This left them "smeared" across the multiverse. Not the ideal afterlife for your parents, but still . . . a bit cosmically romantic. I mean, it is very heroic but not super-great for a little kid who suddenly has no parents. America, bereft and grieving, hastily exited the last portal from the Utopian Parallel into the outer dimensions. She hoped to **TRAVEL THE STARS** and become a hero like her

---

Skills: Natural leader
Hand-to-hand combat
Bilingual
Grade-A flirt

Unofficial Deity: Selena (not Gomez)

Super-powers: Flight
Super-strength
Super-speed
Invulnerability to physical harm (but not to feels)
Interdimensional portal creation
Time travel TBD (she's working on it)

Weaknesses: Oreo ice cream
Cute text messages

mothers. Because America did not have her familia to care for her as she grew up, she was forced to learn to protect herself. She punched first and asked questions later. This made America **TOUGH, RESILIENT, AND FIERCE,** but she still had plenty of lessons to learn about being a hero.

America wandered until she found our Earth, accepting the kindness of strangers to survive. America's home dimension shares striking cultural similarities with Earth's own Latinx community, and because of this she easily found a home on Earth. At just sixteen, America joined the **TEEN BRIGADE** to follow in her mothers' heroic footsteps. Living up to your parents' feats can be hard, especially when you're still just a kid yourself. However, the Teen Brigade didn't last very long, as they parted ways due to "musical differences," aka #DRAMA, not long after. Hey, sometimes it's better to just leave the drama behind, and America still had lots of growing up to do.

Her next team had her joining up with Earth's mightiest teens! America was recruited by a younger and somewhat less-evil-than-usual Loki to join the **YOUNG AVENGERS.** She became best of friends with the magical Wiccan, hulking Hulkling, genius Prodigy, alien bad boy Noh-Varr, and her soon-to-be BFF Kate Bishop (aka the best Hawkeye). Together they faced an interdimensional parasite named Mother that took on the form of the team's (you guessed it) mothers. As you can imagine, this was very hard for America, who had two moms, both of whom are *multiverse smears*. America obviously punched a heap-ton of mothers, eventually banishing the beast and winning the day. But in hopping dimensions and fighting enough mothers to need to have a sit-down with Freud, America realized maybe it was time for her to stop trying to fill her mothers' footsteps and start adulting for real. She took a break from the team to regroup and focus a bit on her solo dreams.

Once the multiverse got back to being less "multi" and more "uni," America got to kicking it with an amazing Super Hero team called the **ULTIMATES,** including the crazy-powerful Blue Marvel, the light-wielding Monica Rambeau, the king himself, Black Panther, and the one-and-only Captain Marvel. She also began dating a super-adorable Earth girl named Lisa Halloran. However, #DRAMA would be back. This time in the form of predictive justice (aka using the visions of an Inhuman named Ulysses to stop violence before it started). The Super Hero community was torn apart with major chaos. Once again it seemed that maybe she needed some solo time.

THE COLLEGE YEARS

America decided after dealing with so much teen (and adult) angst that maybe she should focus on her education. So she did what any red-blooded America would do and signed up for interdimensional Super Hero college at **SOTOMAYOR UNIVERSITY.** Any burgeoning young adult wants to make sure they get the best possible education, and sometimes that means moving far from home. In fact, sometimes that means leaving your dimension altogether to find the school

College Besties: Prodigy, X'Andria, and the ladies in her sorority, LLMPPTB (Leelumultipass Phi Theta Beta)

On-Again/Off-Again Boo: Lisa Halloran

Punch-o-Meter: 11 out of 10 Punches

that is the right fit for your kind of hero. America's main squeeze, **LISA HALLORAN**, saw that they were literally moving apart (like, light-years apart) and ended things. America was heartbroken, but with time and a road trip with her BFF, Kate Bishop, she eventually saw that separating was for the best. And better yet, Lisa and America were able to remain friends after a little distance.

At Sotomayor U, America spent mad hang-time with her boy-genius bud Prodigy and found a new Girl Squad with the ladies of **LLMPPTB**, a sorority of brilliant bad baes. She even was lucky enough to be reunited with her abuela Madrimar. America learned through time travel arranged by her grandmother and her instructor Professor Douglas how to use her head and not just her fists. Traveling back in time to WWII, she was taught by **PEGGY CARTER** how to make a battle plan, and maybe even punched Hitler for Captain America. You go, girl! Then she traveled to Westchester, New York, where Storm taught her to meditate and calm herself during a *storm*. America's newfound ability to focus and plan would soon be put to the test.

The money-grubbing, leather-clad super-freak known as Exterminatrix infiltrated Sotomayor University. She hoped to use America and others to build weaponry for the Midas Foundation. Posing as an administrator and abusing the campus political system, Exterminatrix attempted to lock down and silence the student body. America normally would have gotten angry and started a **SLUG-FEST** she might not have been able to win. After all, Exterminatrix had taken away America and her fellow students' autonomy! And political voice! Not only was that a jerk move, but it was totally dangerous for all the students at Sotomayor! Fortunately, now America knew she had to use her calm and focus if she wanted to conquer this corrupt and abusive system. Using her newfound skills, America was able to expose the leather-clad bad girl's evil plot and punch her back to space. Okay, so maybe you can punch *some* of your problems.

TO PUNCH, OR NOT TO PUNCH, THAT IS THE QUESTION

Soooo . . . America likes to punch her problems. There isn't a battle she can't solve with her fists— or at least that's what she thought for a very long time. However, part of growing up is learning how to keep your lucidity when things are at their worst. Learning how to plan your next moves and breathe through life's difficulties is much, much harder than throwing punches. America is working on her focus through breath, meditation, and using her mind before her muscle. This is greatly aided by leaning on her friends. When in a difficult situation, though America can be a bit of a lone wolf, turning to her friends and mentors for guidance offers her new clarity and perspective to help her win the day. Oh, and it's a lot more fun than dealing with a problem by herself.

Young Avengers Group Chat

America: Check out who I found at Sotomayor U! He's a real PRODIGY!

Kate: OMG! Come visit me!

Noh-Varr: Hello, ladiiiiiieeeeessss.

Wiccan: Hulkling and I are missing you guys!

Loki: New yamblr. Who dis?

America: Dis girl ready to punch you back to Asgard. ;)

QUAKE

FEARLESS LEADER. MOVER. SHAKER.

DAISY JOHNSON is more than an Inhuman Super Hero. She's a stone-cold Agent of S.H.I.E.L.D.* who has been commanding a team of fellow agents since she was a teenager. Not to mention she is the youngest director of S.H.I.E.L.D. ever. Um, back up, did you just register that? Daisy is straight-up **QUAKING THE GLASS CEILING.** Daisy's super-power isn't just using seismic vibrations; her true gift is her confidence in her abilities, and the strong moral compass that guides her decision-making process. This strong sense of right and wrong allows her to assert well-defined boundaries, even when it comes to super-powerful people. It pushes her to question the rules when the rules are wrong—which can be super hard. Her personal conviction alone is enough to shake up any villain. But shake-ups are kind of her thing.

DAISY LOUISE JOHNSON grew up with her adoptive parents, the Suttons, attending high school like any other teenager. . . . Well, until she was recruited by Nick Fury, director of **S.H.I.E.L.D.** Part of Nick Fury's one-of-a-kind recruiting process? Revealing Daisy's true origins. Daisy's biological parents were the deceased Jennifer Johnson and the dangerously trans- forming scientist, Calvin Zabo, who moonlighted as the monstrous Mister Hyde. Learning of her true parentage and her new seismic super-powers, Daisy felt a sense of duty to do what was right. She had a chance to rectify her father's wrongs, avenge her mother's death, and learn how to use her powers to help others. Daisy left school to join **DIRECTOR FURY**. I mean, who says no to Nick Fury, anyway? He has a flying car. (I don't condone leaving high school for a guy with a cool car, just for the record.)

By the age of eighteen, Daisy was a Level 10 Agent with the highest clearance at S.H.I.E.L.D. She was com- pletely off the map until she teamed up with several of Earth's mightiest heroes for a covert mission where Nick Fury conscripted the group to overthrow a corrupt for- eign government. When the secret coup was publicly revealed, Nick Fury was forced to go on the run. Daisy remained with S.H.I.E.L.D., but **MARIA HILL** put her on mandatory retirement at just eighteen years old, which was not as cool as it sounds. Daisy easily could have cracked under the pressure but she knew her loyalty was to Nick Fury and to the mission. She carried it off with a knowing smile and a pile of smugness.

Nick Fury eventually found Daisy. He told her that her next secret mission was to put together a team of gifted young people from Nick's "**CATERPILLAR FILES.**" These recruits were considered "caterpillars"

* S.H.I.E.L.D. stands for Strategic Homeland Intervention, Enforcement, and Logistics Division.

Name: Daisy Louise Johnson	**Super-powers:** Generates seismic vibrations resembling earthquakes (like a QUAKE, get it?) Immune to those vibrations (for the most part . . .)
Aliases: Skye, Quake	
Highest S.H.I.E.L.D. Clearance: Level 10	**Skills:** Leader Martial arts Markswoman Espionage Great poker face

because of their potential to turn into beautiful, butt-kicking butterflies called the Secret Warriors. Daisy enlisted a group of **YOUNG HEROES**, including the fire-chain-wielding Hellfire, the superfast Slingshot, the young god of fear Phobos, the tough-as-bricks Stonewall, and the magic-brandishing Druid. Daisy led her new titanic teenage team to take on a secret invasion by creepy green shape-shifting aliens called Skrulls.

When Nick Fury broke into a S.H.I.E.L.D. base, he found secret files revealing that America's own government had been corrupted by hidden branches of the terrorist organization known as Hydra. Though the Skrulls were on their way out, there was a whole new secret invasion to worry about. Under Nick Fury's tutelage, they uncovered the shadow organization's far-reaching plot to take over the world.

It was more important than ever for Daisy and her team of **SECRET WARRIORS** to remain covert. As a first-time leader, Daisy faced an intense learning curve. No matter her respect for Nick Fury, following anyone blindly can be hard, as it requires a staggering amount of trust. He asked her to remove her teammate Druid as a liability. Daisy pushed back, but Fury removed him anyway. Daisy was frustrated and felt helpless. No one wants to be forced to do anything, much less fire your friend. However, those are the sad and frustrating things that are required when you answer to someone above you.

Daisy's anger and growing involvement with her hot-headed teammate Hellfire (whom she found hot both in temperature and in attractiveness) began to cloud her judgment. Hellfire was more than just a smart-mouthed love interest—he was also an informant for Hydra. The information Daisy shared with him led their team to be ambushed by Hydra on their next mission. During the epic battle, Nick Fury revealed he knew that Hellfire was a double agent and let him fall to his death. The team disbanded.

Can you say *trust issues*?! Hellfire's death and betrayal, Druid's departure, Fury's actions—it was all a lot to take!

Daisy was hurt, furious, and without a team. In a final letter, Fury apologized and encouraged Daisy to build a team her own way. Sometimes when things go upside down, you have to define what you want and what is right for you. Daisy reinstated Druid and welcomed the **HOWLING COMMANDOS** to continue fighting the good fight. Now Daisy could be a leader on her own terms. She took what she learned from Nick Fury, coupled with her own moral code, to make a better, smarter, and stronger team.

Under the weight of the Hydra scandal, S.H.I.E.L.D. fell apart, and a new, more sinister organization named H.A.M.M.E.R. took its place, led by Norman Osborn. During this time, Captain America reinstated S.H.I.E.L.D. in secret, asking Daisy to follow in Nick Fury's footsteps to become the youngest director of the organization in history. OMG! Teenage Daisy Johnson was the leader of S.H.I.E.L.D.—the most powerful covert agency in the world! How flippin' cool is that?!

During her tenure as director, Daisy recruited two of the organization's most famous agents, Nick Fury Jr. and her future mentor, **PHIL COULSON**. Together they took on Norman Osborn's less-than-scrupulous group H.A.M.M.E.R. and returned S.H.I.E.L.D. to its rightful place protecting America. Daisy eventually handed over the title of director to someone with a bit more experience, but she kept S.H.I.E.L.D. afloat when they were facing their greatest threat, and that is unquestionably amazing.

Daisy continued to grow as a hero, fulfilling her lifelong dream of teaming up with the Avengers. **AVENGERS ASSEMBLE!** She aided them against a military-weapon-stealing diplomat, a siege by the gods, and a world-burning cosmic entity.

Daisy later united with S.H.I.E.L.D. agents Phil Coulson, Melinda May, Jemma Simmons, and Leo Fitz. This time Daisy would have to face her literal daddy issues. Daisy's Quake powers began to splinter her bones, and she knew she needed her father's help. His Hyde serum had mixed with her mother's dormant **INHUMAN GENES** to create her Quake powers, and only he knew how to create a cure. As his demure alter ego, the brilliant scientist Calvin Zabo, he was arrested by S.H.I.E.L.D. and charged with making the cure for Daisy. This reawakened his love for his daughter, though Daisy kept a safe distance. He pined to reunite, but she could not trust a man who turned into a literal monster. Calvin did indeed cure Daisy; however, he also attempted to inject her with his maddening Hyde serum. He hoped it would protect her on future missions the way it had protected him as Hyde. But just because your parents want to protect you doesn't mean they are going to go about it the right way. Phil Coulson interceded, using the serum to go fist-to-fist with Zabo, who transformed into Hyde. Using her now-healed vibration powers, Daisy stopped Hyde by opening a crater in the ground that swallowed him up.

Daisy now works with a new team of Secret Warriors, including the shape-shifting Ms. Marvel, the super-

Signature Look: Quake Gauntlets

Mentors: Nick Fury, Phil Coulson

Squads: S.H.I.E.L.D., Inhumans, Avengers, Secret Warriors, Secret Warriors 2.0

Has a Thing for Hotties: Hellfire
Inferno

genius Moon Girl, the calculating Karnak, and the flaming-hot Inferno. (Did I mention she likes hot guys?)

Daisy has learned we cannot choose our parents, but we can choose how we engage with them, and we can choose our families. Sometimes our true family is the friends around us every day. We can lean on mentors like Nick Fury to guide us when no one else can. We can enlist our teammates and friends to help us win our battles and pull out victories. And above all, just because we sometimes **QUAKE**, that does not mean that we are not super-powerful.

SHE-HULK

BUFF BABE. PARTY GIRL. POWER LAWYER.

"**SENSATIONAL**" or "savage": No matter what others call her, we can all agree that **JENNIFER WALTERS** is all She-Hulk. Why do we love her?! Well, let me tell you, Jen doesn't let anyone put limits on what she can do and never gives in to what people think a lady should be. Jen is a brilliant lawyer, a buff Super Hero, and is always the life of the party. This mighty package may be intimidating to some, but Jen knows you can be big, powerful, and an intellectual dynamo that is *all* woman. Hey, people have a lot of ideas about what a lady looks like, and Jen is a reminder that **NO ONE GETS TO TELL YOU WHO YOU ARE**, no matter if you are a boy, girl, nonbinary, actual green person, or any-dang-thing in between. Jen is one of the first ladies to truly show that she doesn't need to be demure or petite to be feminine or foxy. Jen is all about confidence, body positivity, and fun. However, she wasn't always that way (and sometimes still isn't). It takes work.

Jennifer Walters grew up in Los Angeles as a bookish, quiet girl raised by her father, Sheriff Morris Walters, and her mother, Elaine Banner-Walters. (Yeah, Banner as in *that* Banner.) She spent her summers in Charlestown,

Ohio, developing a strong bond with her cousin Bruce Banner. Jen's mother died in a car crash that would later be revealed to be the work of mob boss Nick Trask. Both Jen and her father threw themselves into their work with the law as recompense. Jennifer graduated Harvard to attend law school at UCLA, and was more likely to be hidden in her room studying than hitting the LA party scene (although that would change). Jen was excruciatingly shy at first, but found solace in her work and books.

While working as a lawyer, she took on a case defending a man accused of killing Nick Trask's guard (yeah, the jerk-butt who killed her mom). Seeing that her defendant was framed, she was targeted by the real culprit, Trask, and his henchmen. Trask and his lackeys, trying to stop her, gunned her down. Luckily, her cousin was there and gave her a vital blood transfusion. Unluckily, her cousin is Bruce Banner, the famous scientist who turns into a giant green rage monster called the Hulk. Banner's **GAMMA-IRRADIATED BLOOD** was so genetically similar to Jen's, it combined with her physiology to transform her into the six-foot-seven green glamazon known as **SHE-HULK**. BOOM!

Name: Jennifer Walters	**Super-powers (in Hulk form):** Super-strength
	Enhanced durability
Alias: She-Hulk	Increased endurance
	Healing factor
Nicknames: Jen	Super snacker
Shulkie	
Glamazonia	**Weaknesses:** Radiation
Jade Giantess	Muscular gentlemen
Lady Hulk	Baked goods
Skills: Successful lawyer	**Occupation:** Attorney
Hand-to-hand combat	S.H.I.E.L.D. Agent
Expert pilot	Adventurer

Gal Pals: Hellcat
Weezi
Wasp
Scarlet Witch

Squads: Avengers, Lady Liberators,
Heroes for Hire, A-Force

At first, Jennifer couldn't control her powers as She-Hulk. She would turn green at the worst of times, like during a heated case in court. **BLAM!** All green! But Jen increasingly enjoyed being the Savage She-Hulk. Taking on this persona made her feel **FIERCE AND FORMIDABLE**. Eventually she learned how to control her She-Hulking tendencies, allowing her not only to choose her body's form, but to keep her rational mental state no matter how green she gets. Over time, She-Hulk took down Trask's men, saved the people of Los Angeles from earthquakes and peril, roughed up passing villains like Ultima, Man-Elephant, and Man-Killer, and saved a micro-universe—ya know, like you do. She even met her later BFF, Hellcat!

After so many villains, plus a falling-out with her father and her old friend Zapper, Jen knew it was time for her to get the heck out of LA. She packed up her things and road-tripped to New York City, the home of Super Heroes. There she answered an ad to join the Avengers. Her fellow queen bee of butt-kicking, the Wasp, invited She-Hulk to join alongside Hawkeye—beginning a long, antagonistic friendship between the archer and jade giantess.

While part of the Avengers, Jennifer was pretty much crushing it. Jen was *feeling herself*, and *bringing it* as one of **EARTH'S MIGHTIEST HEROES**. Unfortunately, she would get dragged to a planet called Battleworld by an omnipotent alien named the Beyonder, who wanted to create his very own gladiator-style battles known as the Secret Wars, where Super Heroes and Villains of Earth faced off. During this time, She-Hulk started an ongoing feud with the original mean gargantuan girl, Titania, who was as strong as she was not nice. Though Titania and Shulkie could have been buff girl BFFs, Titania was

obsessed with besting the green glam machine. Jen was forced to face off against Titania again and again—even long after they were free of the Beyonder and returned to Earth.

Back home in New York City, Jennifer really came into her own. She got a job at a district attorney's office, where she met her girl, Louise "Weezi" Grant-Mason—aka the **BLONDE PHANTOM**. The ladies loved going on adventures together, whether they were zipping back and forth to LA in Jen's totally awesome flying car to see her father or punching out bad guys. But She-Hulk wasn't just spending quality time with Weezi—she also got into the habit of directly addressing her readers and occasionally tearing through the pages of the comics as people read them. She-Hulk is a woman who is hard to contain.

You called? Oh boy, here we go again. Hi, Shulkie! **Hey, girl! You know, way before Gwenpool was even born, I was jumping into the white space and chatting with readers. Hey, reader!** That's great. You've inspired future generations, it seems. **All in a day's work for Shulkie! Also, does anyone have a snack? I am famished! This much muscle requires fuel. Just toss something into these pages.** PLEASE DON'T TRY TO SHOVE SNACKS INTO THIS BOOK. **Fine, I'll go ask Thor. Asgardian snacks are HEAVENLY.** As I was saying . . .

Jennifer was loving working for the DA and rocking that #HeroLife while living at Avengers Mansion.

THE BLONDE PHANTOM

Considered to be the first woman introduced as a Marvel Super Hero, the Blonde Phantom splashed onto comic-book pages as the petite and modest secretary Louise Grant. At night, she took on the masked moniker the Blonde Phantom, using her natural athletic ability and detective skills to solve crimes big and small.

However, Jen's lifestyle became a problem. She partied too hard and was eventually let go from the DA's office *and* asked to move out of the Mansion by Captain A-stick-in-the-mud-ica, who didn't appreciate her rowdy parties or overnight guests. Admittedly, it's probably not a great idea to invite strangers into a home full of special weapons, government secrets, and heroes who have Super Villains looking for them. Fortunately, Jen was offered a job at the prestigious law firm Goodman, Lieber, Kurtzberg, and Holliway. However, the big boss didn't want She-Hulk parading through their offices or bringing her party girl persona. This was kind of a bummer for her, because Jen generally prefers to don her muscular green appearance—it makes her feel confident, sexy, and charismatic.

But Jen had to get used to not having a big, powerful persona to hide behind and to be comfortable with her vulnerable, smaller body—one she couldn't use to pound her problems into submission. She had to use her mind first, which was especially important when she began working with her rival and frenemy Mallory Book. Mallory could be prickly and hurtful, but Jen had to take the high road and prove her powerfulness by winning her cases. Luckily, she had the help of the kindhearted Augustus "Pug" Pugliese. Together, the team took on cases of super-powered clients who needed protection and monetary reimbursement. Jen learned to help out the little guy—and herself—in her own vulnerable form.

Eventually, Jen took a little time off-planet to administer some intergalactic justice and do some heavy training with the toughest Guardian of the Galaxy, Gamora. After three months of training, She-Hulk's strength increased so much that she had to wear a power-dampening ensemble called the **JUPITER SUIT**, and learned how to use her strength without crushing everything.

Jennifer also hooked up with some awesome lady teams, including the **LADY LIBERATORS** and a team of Avengers made up of women called **A-FORCE**.

> **Fun Fact:** Three of the namesakes of the legendary law firm of Goodman, Lieber, Kurtzberg, and Holliway are all legendary comic-book creators: Goodman is Martin Goodman, the original publisher of Marvel Comics; Lieber is the real name of the iconic Stan Lee; and Kurtzberg was Jacob Kurtzberg, or as many better know him, the prolific comic-book creator Jack Kirby. Although Holliway isn't a real-life comics pro, he's still important—he's the character who hires Jennifer in the comics.

But hey, **LIFE ISN'T ALL SUNSHINE, PUPPIES, AND HULKING OUT.** She almost died during a battle with the intergalactic, death-obsessed alien Thanos, leaving her traumatized and literally gray. Jen has been spending more time getting to know and taking care of her non-Hulk self, working on cases to help super-people, finding ways to manage her new anxiety, and watching a lot of baking videos. Whatever helps, right? One day at a time, Jen healed. It wasn't long before Jen was back on her feet, greener than ever, and already giving major flirty vibes to Thor Odinson. What can I say? You can't keep a good Shulkie down.

THOR

FIRST, let me explain how there are two Thors. Thor Odinson is the brawny, hunky male Thor, and **JANE FOSTER** transforms into the brawny, babely goddess Thor. For purposes of clarity, I will call Jane Foster "Thor" and male Thor "Odinson." You with me? **FOR ASGARD!** (That means *Great!*)

Jane Foster wasn't always a god. She started out as a normal human, just like any one of us. She became a nurse and worked her way up to being a full-fledged doctor, which already basically makes her a hero on two counts. However, Jane was pulled into the world of Super Heroes and would eventually follow the call to become one herself.

Jane Foster was working as a nurse alongside sickly doctor Donald Blake, who happened to transform into Thor Odinson when he struck his cane on the ground. Jane would often be caught up in the shenanigans of Odinson and Dr. Donald Blake, crushing on both of them but unaware they were in fact **THE SAME GUY.** And this wasn't any of that silly just-putting-on-a-pair-of-sunglasses stuff. His body, face, and whole persona fully transformed into his alter ego—the God of Thunder. The love triangle between Donald, Jane, and Odinson

became even more tricky when you consider the **ALL-FATHER, ODIN**, did not approve of gods dating plain old humans.

Odinson's father protested, but it did not keep Odinson from wanting to put a ring on it. He brought Jane to the godly realm of Asgard to meet the fam and hopefully earn her a spot in the heavens once and for all. Odin agreed to give Jane a chance to become a god (which was not all that likely, considering she had little opportunity to do well—-the King of the Gods had his own agenda). Odin turned Jane into the goddess of flight, and put her through a series of tests. Odin wasn't playing fair, though, and set Jane up to fail. When she did, Odin sent her back to Earth. Odinson was forbidden from seeing Jane any longer. Her mind was wiped clean of Odinson, and life continued. Pretty easy breakup for her, really.

Jane and Odinson moved on, but when Jane was on the verge of death, an unexpected goddess came to help. Odinson's long-intended Asgardian love, Sif, came to Jane's aid. Their bodies were fused together. For a while Sif and Jane shared a body, not unlike Donald Blake and Odinson had previously. This was honestly kind of weird, because they both dated Odinson, but sometimes

---

Name: Jane Foster

Alias: Thor

BFFs: Mjolnir, Agent Rosalind "Roz" Solomon, Freya

Skills: Medical doctor
Can handle a lot of Super Hero drama

Super-powers (as Thor): Godly strength
Godly durability
Super-speed
Flight
Super-stamina
Teleportation
Energy projection
Weather manipulation

Allspeak (can speak all languages)
Mental link with Mjolnir

Fun Fact: Jane Foster's rise to godhood was first foreshadowed in a comic called *What If . . . ?* where writers experimented with one-off stories outside of continuity (basically sanctioned fan fiction). In one issue they asked the question "What if Jane Foster had found the hammer of Thor?" The answer? She finds the hammer instead of Donald Blake to become the goddess Thordis. She bests a ton of baddies, but her beloved Donald Blake falls for the goddess Sif while Thordis is away. As a consolation prize, Jane ends up marrying Odin and is crowned queen of the gods, which is pretty weird when you consider the age difference between Jane and Odin, and that they just met, and the whole "boyfriend's dad" thing. Luckily, the next time we see Jane as Thor, things shake out a little differently.

dating a dude can really bring two women closer. Like . . . much, much closer—literally.

The ladies eventually separated bodies, and Jane married Dr. Donald Blake's rival, Keith Kincaid. Jane furthered her medical education. She helped out the Avengers alongside Keith. However, their relationship deteriorated when she heard that Odinson had returned. She hoped to rekindle her relationship with the God of Thunder.

Jane Foster became an ER doctor, continuing to help out the Avengers between patients and finding tenuous romance with Odinson. **#ITSCOMPLICATED**. However, the doctor would soon become the patient. Jane was diagnosed with breast cancer that was both aggressive and malignant. Odinson offered Jane the role of Senator for **MIDGARD** (Midgard is what those wacky Asgardians call Earth) in the Congress of Worlds. Though Jane was sick, she accepted. She felt a deep sense of duty as someone who was very familiar not just with

Earth but with the many realms that Odinson traveled. Like Jane, we should all take an interest in our world and advocate to make it better.

Not long after, Odinson fell from grace, becoming unworthy of his hammer, **MJOLNIR**. The hammer chose Jane as the person most worthy to wield it, transforming her into the blond badass **GODDESS OF THUNDER**. As Thor, she was compelled to protect the ten realms from various Frost Giants, Dark Elves, and the king Odin himself, when warranted. However, Jane's

On-Again/Off-Again Boos: Thor
Keith Kincaid
Sam Wilson

Enemies: Loki
Odin
Frost Giants
Malekith the Accursed

Realms: Midgard (Earth)
Asgardia (New Asgard)

time as the Goddess of Thunder left her human body even more weak and frail. She began missing her cancer treatments to answer the call of Thor, and her body began faltering in battle. And what was worse, Odin really never liked her taking the mantle of Thor from his son.

Odin sent his big cruel brother, Cul Borson—the God of Fear—to take back Thor's hammer. What's worse, he was wearing the Destroyer armor, which is a big, gnarly suit that could crush a city. With the help of the **ALL-MOTHER, FREYA** (a goddess in her own right), plus a band of warrior women, and Odinson himself, Thor defeated the Destroyer armor. This obviously didn't sit well with Odin. He became enraged and mad with power, and took his wife, Freya, as his prisoner, declaring her to be guilty of treason. While Freya was on trial, Thor interrupted the proceedings to free her. In the past, Odin had stopped Jane's relationship with Odinson. He never found her worthy. And now here she was, Thor herself, the worthiest of all! She could finally fight back. Plus, she was punching him across the cosmos, so that felt pretty darn fulfilling. (It sure beats cancer, anyway.)

In the midst of this war, a new battle began when Malekith the Accursed, leader of the Dark Elves, waged a war across the realms. Loki, the God of Mischief, was, OF COURSE, playing both sides as a double agent (he's the flippin' god of MISCHIEF). He stabbed his own adoptive mother, Freya, with a poison blade. This immediately stopped the fight between Thor and Odin, as Odin rushed to Freya's side to heal her. The brutish Cul Borson took the throne in Odin's place. Asgard would have to survive under his brutish rule until Odin and Freya emerged.

Things weren't any simpler for Jane in her human form! Her transformations between human and goddess Thor interrupted her chemotherapy treatments, and **S.H.I.E.L.D.** began hounding her as a potentially super-powered person and alter ego to Thor. Luckily her new friend, S.H.I.E.L.D. Agent Roz Solomon,

MJOLNIR

Thor's hammer, Mjolnir, can conduct thunder and lightning, open portals, and make her fly in addition to obviously being a powerful weapon. But the hammer also once came to Jane when she was most in need and took on the appearance of Thor herself! It allowed Jane to hide her secret identity from S.H.I.E.L.D., and it even healed a lethal bullet wound. Pretty handy for a hammer!

helped her hide this. After all, they both dated Odinson, and knew that being Thor was complicated business. Furthermore, the ladies learned they could be an asset to each other as they fought crimes Asgardian and otherwise.

Thor also joined the **ALL-NEW, ALL-DIFFERENT AVENGERS** to help protect the Earth, where she started a flirt-a-thon with Sam Wilson, aka Falcon (although at the time he was filling in as Captain America). After a successful mission, feeling the heat of the moment and knowing that she must live her life to the fullest, she grabbed Sam and kissed him. With her body ailing, Jane knew now more than ever that she must enjoy things while they happen. Live for today, because you never know what tomorrow may hold.

Though Jane would ultimately have to choose between her time as Thor and allowing her body to heal as Jane, she continues to be a woman strong enough to know when to care for herself so she may care for others.

On Mjolnir it reads, **"WHOSOEVER HOLDS THIS HAMMER, IF SHE BE WORTHY, SHALL POSSESS THE POWER OF THOR."** Jane was chosen because she is worthy. You may not have a hammer that says it, but you are worthy, too.

SCIENCE SQUAD

IN THESE PAGES, prepare to meet some of Marvel's greatest scientific minds! From Lunella Lafayette, the smartest person in the world, to the S.H.I.E.L.D. research scientist Mockingbird, to Riri Williams, the fifteen-year-old dynamo who reverse engineered her own Iron Man armor—these ladies have got **STEM** on lock! Let's do some research of our own, shall we?

G.I.R.L.
Scientific Research Collective

This badass lab was founded by **NADIA VAN DYNE** with the help of her stepmother, Janet Van Dyne! In Nadia's own words, G.I.R.L. (Genius In action Research Labs) is "dedicated to finding the brilliant girls and women who will not just save the world, but change it." LaShayla "Shay" Smith, Priya Aggarwal, Taina Miranda, and Ying (G.I.R.L.'s faithful members) are housed at **PYM LABS**, where Nadia works in her father Hank Pym's old laboratory. (You might remember him as the original Ant-Man.) In addition, the lab has some of the greatest research tech around. It has also been outfitted with dorm rooms for the girls and their overseeing scientist, Mockingbird, aka the legendary S.H.I.E.L.D. agent/scientist/adventurer Bobbi Morse!

XIAOYI "ISO" CHEN
Engineer, Terrigen Expert

Iso, a New Inhuman, is a mechanical and engineering genius. She was selected by the Inhuman Queen Medusa to work on a cure for a disease plaguing mutants. A huge job for a **BURGEONING SCIENTIST!** Iso was more than up to the task. Especially when you consider her Inhuman ability to control pressure systems. You might even say Iso works best under pressure.

VIVIAN "VIV" VISION
Synthezoid Technology Expert

Imagine if you had a friend who emitted Wi-Fi! Viv is the ultimate technological mind, because she IS technology. When her father, Vision, found himself single but ready to settle down, he just created an **ANDROID FAMILY** of his own. Viv is a microchip off the old block with a brain out of a **SUPER COMPUTER!** She comes complete with internet access and a search engine at the ready. No wonder she knows it all!

DR. WILMA CALVIN
S.H.I.E.L.D. Biochemist

Meet one of Marvel's earliest notable scientists who has been breaking barriers for **WOMEN OF COLOR** in STEM since 1972! Dr. Wilma Calvin was assisted by none other than Bobbi Morse in her early days as a scientist. This position would later inspire Bobbi to become one of S.H.I.E.L.D.'s greatest agents—Mockingbird. Wilma also uncovered the greatest secrets of the **SUPER-SOLDIER SERUM** that gave Captain America his famed strength. Dr. Calvin has created the serum's closest approximation since its inception with her work for **"PROJECT: GLADIATOR."**

ELSA BLOODSTONE
Archaeologist, Monster Hunter

This straight-shooting Brit was born into a long line of **MONSTER HUNTERS**, which means she doesn't like to just track down horrific beasts, she studies them, too! In order to pursue these oft-antediluvian beings, she has become an expert in ancient civilizations, dead languages, folklore, and monster biology. All of which she uses to track down malicious creatures and obliterate them. Her achievements have even landed her a professorship at the **BRADDOCK ACADEMY** in her home country of Great Britain.

ANNA MARIA MARCONI
Chemistry, Physics, and Cybernetics Specialist

Though some may underestimate her due to her small stature, Anna Maria Marconi is a genuine scientific genius. She first met Peter Parker while he was finishing his doctorate. (He was actually under the control of the villain Doctor Octopus at the time, but let's not worry too much about that.) She became his chemistry and physics tutor. Yes, she straight-up schooled Spider-Man! She was immediately hired by Parker Industries, where she became one of the world's most advanced research scientists. She even helped Doctor Octopus take on more **HEROIC CYBERNETIC WORKS**, which she continued after his control over Peter Parker's body ceased.

MOON GIRL
Genius Inventor

Though Lunella Lafayette is only nine years old, she is the **SMARTEST PERSON ON EARTH!** Her Super Hero name, Moon Girl, was originally what her peers used to mockingly call her, for her love of space. She's still just a kid, but her youthful imagination often results in ingenious inventions adults might never even consider! From her spring-loaded skates to her fully functioning cybernetic Lego triceratops, Lunella never limits her creativity. Oh, and she's even been featured as a guest speaker at the interdimensional Super Hero college **SOTOMAYOR UNIVERSITY!**

IRONHEART
Advance Technologies

Riri Williams's true superpower is her **GENIUS** as an engineer. Graduating high school at fifteen years old, she headed off to college at MIT where she was able to reverse engineer her own Iron Man armor in the school lab. With the blessing of Tony Stark and added bonus of her own personal Stark Artificial Intelligence system, Riri now fights crime as Ironheart. She continues to improve the functionality of her Ironheart tech, because any machine can always be **BETTER, FASTER, AND SMARTER.**

BLACK WIDOW

SUPER-SPY. ASSASSIN. ABSOLUTELY LETHAL.

SOME MIGHT find Natasha Romanoff cold, but she grew up in a cold place, during a Cold War, and was trained to be a stone-cold assassin. Cold is in her blood. Nat isn't here to smile and make you feel good, unless that is her assignment. If a guy asked Natasha to smile as she walked by, she'd probably Tase him with one of her **WIDOW'S BITES**. She *is* here to get the job done quickly, quietly, and well. Though she may not be the softest and cuddliest of women, Nat is without a doubt someone who cares profoundly . . . though it may be hard to see at first glance. She has been through a great deal of trauma in her life, but she has allowed that trauma to help her grow and become a better person.

NATASHA was born in Russia. After the death of her mother, she was raised by the **KGB'S BLACK WIDOW PROGRAM**. There, in a facility named the Red Room, Natasha was trained to be a spy, an assassin, an acrobat, and a master of deceit. She also was instructed as a prima ballerina, though it appears some of those memories may have been implanted by the KGB. This is how a great deal of Natasha's memories feel—like they may or may not be real or her own. Many have played with her mind, and as you can imagine this can be hard to cope with at times, even for a master assassin.

During her time in the **KGB'S RED ROOM**, she trained with the Winter Soldier, who also moonlighted as Captain America's BFF, Bucky Barnes, before his capture and subsequent brainwashing. Natasha and Bucky had a brief kindling of a relationship before it was arranged for her to marry a Russian fighter pilot named Alexei Shostakov. Though not long after their marriage Alexei was reported to have died in a test flight crash, he would resurface in Natasha's life more than once.

In her early missions, Natasha was sent with her fellow agent Boris Turgenov to Tony Stark's laboratory in search of a defected scientist named Professor Anton Vanko. Her job was to distract ladies' man Tony Stark while Boris recovered the professor. However, the mission soon went south when Boris got into one of Vanko's armors, and both the professor and Boris were Vanko-uished in its destruction. (Too soon?) Natasha made a run for it, knowing that a failed mission might cost her life.

Name: Natasha Romanoff

Aliases: Natalia Romanova, Nat, the Black Widow

Bases: Avengers Mansion
S.H.I.E.L.D. HQ

Super-powers: None (but she was given a Russian serum that improves her healing and immune system, and slows her aging process)

Skills: Ballet
Acrobatics
Martial arts
Multilingual
Markswoman
Computer hacking
Espionage
Weapons expert
Master tactician
Seduction and manipulation

Glare-o-Meter: 12 out of 10 glares

In time Natasha hoped that she might leave Russia and be accepted into the ranks of **THE AVENGERS** alongside her new lover, the straight-shooting archer Hawkeye. However, Nick Fury had other plans and recruited Nat into the covert agency **S.H.I.E.L.D.** With the impressive success of her first mission, she proved herself more than capable as a member of S.H.I.E.L.D. and the Avengers. During this time Natasha went back and forth between being an Avenger and an Agent of S.H.I.E.L.D., eventually splitting with Hawkeye but remaining his friend.

Natasha would later team up both heroically and romantically with the hero of Hell's Kitchen, **DAREDEVIL**. The two moved to San Francisco together to fight crime, eat Rice-A-Roni, and ride cable cars. Natasha also got a side hustle as a fashion designer. Though their partnership was fruitful, Natasha ultimately would leave him because he didn't treat her as an equal on the battlefield. Natasha doesn't have time for a guy who doesn't think she can keep up. Doesn't he realize she's the Black-flippin'-Widow?! Nat knows it's important to have a partner who believes in you, and who you believe in, too. Case closed.

Natasha would spend a little time in LA. She cofounded a team called **THE CHAMPIONS** and

Important Beaus: Alexei Shostakov (Red Guardian), Hawkeye, Daredevil, Winter Soldier, Hercules

Squads: K.G.B.
Avengers
S.H.I.E.L.D.
Secret Avengers
Champions
Lady Liberators

ACCESSORIES TO DIE FOR

Black Widow's gauntlets are dangerous weapons that project various tools such as Widow's Bites, which electrocute the target; Widow's Kiss, which contains a powerful knockout drug; and Widow's Line, which can be used for rappelling up the side of a building; in addition to other items such as tear gas. Her signature belt contains explosive discs of TNT as well as other weapons, such as knives. She's one girl who's got it all.

hooked up with the musclebound god Hercules before heading back to NYC. There, she continued working for S.H.I.E.L.D. and teaming up with the Avengers. Although Natasha is a fab Avenger, Agent, and Champion, she really works best alone.

Going solo from both the Avengers and Hercules, Natasha defeated an army, saved her mentor, Ivan Petrovitch Bezukhov, saved her former husband, Alexei (who turned out to be a **LIFE MODEL DECOY**), stopped the rebirth of an epic villain, died, came back to life, and overcame Russian reprogramming. She had a little help along the way, but she had to do it all with her own grit. Natasha finally returned to the Avengers and became the team's coleader alongside the moody, armor-wearing Black Knight. Girl was buuuuuuusy.

Natasha continued working alongside S.H.I.E.L.D. and the Avengers until she was reunited with someone from her early life in Russia—the Winter Soldier. Bucky first reentered her life still brainwashed and trying to take down the Avengers. In time, he shook off his old programming and turned over a new leaf, working with the Avengers as a hero and even filling in for Captain America for a short time. There was a tenderness between Bucky and Natasha that rekindled. The two had undergone so much brainwashing by both the KGB and S.H.I.E.L.D. that relationships with other people were hard to keep stable. However, there was always immense understanding and fondness between the two, as few could comprehend their lives as well as they do. They are the only two that can truly understand each other's lives and experiences.

The Black Widow again went her own way, taking espionage jobs and wiping out the red in her ledger from her past mistakes. We all make mistakes as we learn, and some are worse than others. Sometimes we hurt people without realizing the repercussions of our actions. Natasha is not defined by her guilt, but she is driven by her regrets to make amends. Also, she can break a guy's neck with her thighs. But, yeah, she's also trying really hard to be a better person.

Natasha demonstrated her growth when she intercepted a fatal blow at the hands of the evil organization Hydra to protect the teenage hero **MILES MORALES**, aka Spider-Man. She was seriously hurt in the process, but soon reappeared after Hawkeye and Winter Soldier teamed up to find her. It's hard to keep a good spy down.

Fun Fact: So, did I mention there is more than one Black Widow? Probably a good time to note that the Red Room produced several such women, including Natasha's rival, Yelena Belova. First, the two faced off to find Nick Fury's Super-Soldier Serum, and then they literally faced off by removing their faces. On a mission for S.H.I.E.L.D., Natasha surgically swapped faces with Yelena Belova. Yelena didn't handle this so well. As Yelena, Natasha infiltrated the KGB, and after getting what she wanted, Natasha swapped back her and Yelena's faces. Ouch!

SPIDER-WOMAN

AVENGER. DETECTIVE. SUPER-MOM.

JESSICA DREW might have an alias that's similar to another web-slinger's, but she's a hero all her own! In addition to the wall-crawling super-powers like that spider-guy, Jessica Drew can emit **VENOM BLASTS** from her hands like supercharged Tasers. She can give off powerful pheromones that make people scared of or attracted to her. (She almost never abuses this power, unless you count that time she used her pheromones to convince the Hulk to make her a sandwich, which honestly was a very good cause.) But perhaps most impressive of all, Jessica has learned to have a good sense of humor about things. She has been through her fair share of brainwashing, kidnapping, manipulation, and gaslighting. Despite this fact, Jessica has learned to trust, leaning hard on the friendship of her fellow lady Avengers, and of course finding love in the most unexpected places. More on that soon.

Jessica didn't exactly have your average childhood. British research scientists Miriam and Jonathan Drew worked in the small European range of the **WUNDAGORE MOUNTAINS**, collecting and studying various breeds of spiders for genetic experimentation. While pregnant with Jessica, her mother, Miriam, was caught in the ray of the genome-manipulation machine.

Jessica was born seemingly healthy, but unbeknownst to Miriam, Jessica's father, Jonathan, began experimenting on her, under the guise that it was a "treatment." Not cool, Dad!

Miriam realized Jonathan's true intent and intervened—like a **TRUE HERO**. However, when Jonathan lashed out at them, Jessica manifested Venom Blasts from her hands for the first time, knocking both of her parents unconscious. Jessica passed out and was taken by her father's research benefactor, a genetic modification–obsessed scientist who would come to be known as the High Evolutionary. You can guess why. Despite being an evolutionary, he was hardly highly evolved in his treatment of others.

When she awoke, ten years had passed, and her abilities had been evolved (you can guess by who). She was introduced to the seemingly altruistic organization Hydra, where she was further brainwashed. At the Hydra base, she fell in love with a young, handsome recruit named Jared while they were training to become agents. However, when Jared was taken prisoner by the organization **S.H.I.E.L.D.**, Jessica went to save her man. In the skirmish, a literal switch went off and a video of Hydra's true operations played. Hydra was actually a

---

Name: Jessica Drew

Aliases: Spider-Woman, Arachne, Web-lady

Skills: Martial arts
Tactician
Skilled investigator
Multilingual
Espionage

Super-powers: Wall-crawling
Venom Blasts
Pheromone secretion
Super-strength
Speed
Reflexes
Durability
Healing factor
Winged glide

terrorist organization. Jessica was shocked, and what wounded deeper was that Jared revealed himself as a plant meant to manipulate her; he never loved her. Jessica, horrified and furious, and confused about what was real, returned to the Hydra base and destroyed it.

Jessica went on the run. She bounced between London and Los Angeles and San Francisco working as a secret Super Hero, bounty hunter, and detective and doing her best to outrun Hydra. During this time, as the hero **SPIDER-WOMAN** she saved Carol Danvers (later to be known as the hero Captain Marvel), who nearly fell off the Golden Gate Bridge. The powerful ladies began a lifelong friendship.

A tougher road was still ahead. An encounter with the ancient sorceress Morgan Le Fay would remove some of Jessica's powers and even leave her bodiless (aka pretty dead) until the Avengers defeated the malicious magician and Jessica was returned to her body by Doctor Strange. For a while Jessica remained depowered, and other Spider-Women filled in for her while **MADAME WEB** helped Jessica regain her powers.

> Fun Fact: Jessica's longtime costume was actually made for her by the terrorist organization Hydra. When Jessica went on the run, she took her specialty suit, which helped her control and channel her powers as well as glide on the air with her special webbed wings.

NEW DO

Jessica is a natural blonde, but went brunette to hide her secret identity. So, as the age-old question goes . . . do blondes have more fun? Clearly, the answer is dependent on your desire to hide your identity and your roots.

When Hydra approached Jessica to become a double agent to infiltrate S.H.I.E.L.D., Jessica took this informa-tion to S.H.I.E.L.D. Director Nick Fury, who encouraged her to accept and inform for S.H.I.E.L.D. instead. Unfor-tunately, the Hydra agents were actually bodysnatching aliens called Skrulls, who replaced Jessica with their queen in order to start a secret invasion of Earth. Tony Stark found Jessica along with other kidnapped and replaced heroes, but Jessica was not okay. So much of her life had been taken from her. So much was out of her control. To reclaim power over her life, she worked with **S.W.O.R.D.** (the Sentient World Observation and Response Department), hunting down the dang invading Skrulls and making sure what happened to her would never happen to others.

Squads: Hydra
S.H.I.E.L.D.
New Avengers
Avengers
Lady Liberators
S.W.O.R.D.

Family: Jonathan Drew (Dad)
Miriam Drew (Mom)
Gerry Drew (Son)

In time, Jessica headed back to Earth to rejoin **THE AVENGERS**, but her travels through the Marvel Universe were hardly over. She helped to stop a siege on the godly realm of **ASGARD**. (You're welcome, Thor.) And she later teamed up with every spider-person in every dimension to fight off spider-consuming creeps named the Inheritors. Jessica had more than filled up her passport.

Jessica then took a step back from the Avengers, focusing more on her previous career as a private investigator. She wanted to have greater impact on the lives of the people she was trying to protect. Furthermore, she finally reached a point in her life where she was feeling mentally healthy and ready to have a child. Because she wasn't in a meaningful relationship, she decided to be artificially inseminated. She was ready for more, so she took control of the situation. Jessica continued working, but she knew she needed help with her practice and bringing up a baby. It takes a village—or at least Midtown. She brought on a reformed D-List villain, the Porcupine, aka Roger Gocking, and investigative journalist Ben Urich to assist with her cases. And when her son, **GERRY DREW**, was born, they assisted with babysitting duties.

As a baby, Gerry manifested spider-like powers like his mother's, including climbing walls, increased strength, Venom Blasts, and probably too much fearlessness. Luckily, Jessica's BFF, Captain Marvel, provided

Gerry with a special alien crib called a **VOLDURIAN INCUBATION FIELD**, which could contain his superhuman antics. Good thing Jess had as much support as she did!

Seeing Roger's devotion not only to her son, but to Jessica herself, Jessica's feelings for him began to blossom. Who could resist his messy hair, handsome beard, and gentle affection with her son? Though some of her hero friends initially protested (Roger was known to be a bit of a jerk as the Porcupine), they were soon won over. Her new boyfriend Roger was an ex-criminal after all, but technically so was Jessica. Just because someone makes a mistake does not mean they cannot be reformed and live a good life. Roger turned over a new leaf when he came to work for Jess, and ended up as her manny. When her super pals saw to what lengths Roger would go to care for her son, they welcomed him with open arms.

Although Jessica initially felt guilty about doing Super Hero work when she could be spending more time with Gerry, she ultimately realized that the best thing for her son was to teach him by example and show him how important it is to use her gifts to better the world. After all, mothers are more than just parents: they are women with dreams, career ambitions, friendships, and worlds to save. Gerry is fortunate to get to see his mother as more than just the person who cares for him, but as a human being who cares for the world as a true hero.

Jessica Drew is proof that no matter your past, present, or even predestined future, you can make life what you want it to be. From leaving her Hydra beginnings behind to choosing a heroic profession more in line with her values to her choice to start a family of her own when she was ready, Jessica knows that if you surround yourself with good people and you work hard, **YOU CAN ACCOMPLISH ANYTHING**.

MARY JANE WATSON

CELEBRITY. CLUB CONNOISSEUR. ENTREPRENEUR.

TO THE UNINITIATED, Mary Jane might seem like little more than a love interest for Peter Parker, aka Spider-Man, but I'm here to tell you that's only half the story. Don't confuse how people might feel about Mary Jane with who Mary Jane really is. **MARY JANE WATSON** is defined by her confidence and self-respect. She has always known her worth and has never sacrificed her ambition for any relationship.

Taking on careers as a model, actress, nightclub owner, and businesswoman, she has shown that she knows how to hustle and be her own breadwinner. Mary Jane won't be waiting by the phone for any fella. She has refused many a suitor because she had her eye on the prize, valuing her career and freedom over romantic entanglements. That being said, when Mary Jane loves someone, she is willing to make sacrifices as a devoted friend and partner. Mary Jane proves you really can have it all!

Men are drawn to Mary Jane not just because of her external beauty, but because she suffers no fools and loves herself too much to do anything less than exactly what she wants. She isn't playing hard to get, she *is* hard to get, because she knows her value. Mary Jane Watson doesn't settle—and that is truly intoxicating. We could all be a bit more like Mary Jane.

"FACE IT, TIGER. YOU JUST HIT THE JACKPOT." These were the first words Mary Jane ever said to **PETER PARKER**, and they truly encapsulate the essence of this self-assured and dynamic dame. When Mary Jane was a girl, her parents had split, so she enjoyed staying with her Aunt Anna in Forest Hills, Queens, next door to Aunt May, Peter's aunt. Her turbulent home life had resulted in frequent moves, which left Mary Jane with a rare perspective on the impermanence of life and a need to seem okay to the outside world. Instead of drawing inward, Mary Jane became a sassy, hilarious, flirty young woman who was always the life of the party.

Their aunts often tried to set the two up, but Peter refused, wrongfully assuming Mary Jane would be a weirdo. When she finally appeared in his doorway, Peter was shocked to find that Mary Jane was a popular, carefree girl who delighted in not belonging to anyone or anything. Too often, her detached attitude was wrongly viewed as frivolous instead of life-affirming, but no one could deny that Mary Jane was always gregarious. Mary Jane was all about living for the now, because who knows where tomorrow might take you?

Though Peter and Mary Jane dated a bit casually in their high school years, he was too serious for young Mary Jane. However, after the death of her dear friend

---

Skills: Actress
Model
Negotiator
Businesswoman
Life of any party

Super-powers: Patience with Peter Parker
Can flirt with anything

**Nicknames for
Attractive Fellas:** "Handsome"
"Tiger"
"Brown eyes"

GWEN STACY, with whom Peter was romantically involved, MJ insisted on helping her friend Peter through the mourning process.

Though MJ developed feelings for Peter, she wouldn't give in to a romantic relationship with him because she wanted to focus on her future. Besides, he was still reeling from Gwen Stacy's death, as was she. Mary Jane recognized that he needed a friend because of his deep depression and self-inflicted isolation. This shared mourning brought them together, and from that closeness came something more. As Peter said good-bye before he left for a short trip to Paris, an unexpected and very electric kiss left them forever changed.

As Mary Jane and Peter began to date, she was basically a saint for not ripping off his full head. In the early days, he wasn't open about being a vigilante dressed like a spider, so he was ghosting her 24/7. Sure, Mary Jane is a FREE-SPIRITED GAL, but the seeming lack of respect Peter had for her, coupled with his running off at the drop of a hat, did not go unnoticed. Mary Jane made it clear to him what was acceptable behavior. She demanded Peter's respect and he gave it in any way he could.

Peter eventually proposed to MJ. Though she considered it, she returned the ring. She had more men to date and more life to live before she'd be ready to settle down, if at all. After her sister's disastrous marriage right after high school and her parents' own divorce, she did not want to make the same mistakes. All of this was waaaay

too heavy, so she left New York for a while to work on her modeling career and reconnect with her family. If their love was meant to be, it could certainly withstand some time for them to grow up.

Mary Jane returned to NYC and revealed that she knew about Peter's secret identity all along. SURPRISE! I mean it was kind of hard for her not to know at that point, with him constantly disappearing. Peter and MJ fell back into their old rhythm and back into their old love, this time with more openness, communication, and maturity. Peter proposed again and she finally accepted, despite every eligible bachelor in New York City trying to convince her to stop the wedding.

Although their marriage was happy, Mary Jane's success as a model and actress intimidated Peter. However, she did not allow her husband's insecurities to impede her own ambitions. She supported herself and Peter while doing what she loved every day. She transitioned from modeling to acting. Mary Jane took a role on the hit daytime drama *Secret Hospital*. She even fought for her role to be adjusted to be less vapid and mean, and a more three-dimensional woman. GET IT, MJ!

Mary Jane and Peter had some rough patches, as Mary Jane dealt with the pressures of her career and the worry that she could become a widow if Peter's Spider-Man activities landed him in harm's way. However, they were truly thrilled when Mary Jane announced her pregnancy. Things seemed on the way up as Peter made promises to prioritize his family over Super Hero activities and another hero stepped in to take his place. But tragedy struck when she was poisoned by one of Peter's enemies, causing her to lose the baby. This is an enormous and painful loss for any excited parent. The couple soldiered on, but the mourning was deep and painful. Miscarriage and stillbirth often aren't talked about because of their profound sadness, but Peter and Mary Jane were there for each other through everything. Room for acknowledgment and mourning together was so important for both of them.

OTP: Mary Jane + Peter Parker

College: Empire State University

Interests: Fashion
Acting
Business
Travel

But even more trouble was ahead. Mary Jane and Peter Parker would finally face a problem they could not handle. Peter's Aunt May lay dying and the demon Mephisto gave the couple the option to save her if they agreed to allow the demon to go back in time and erase their entire marriage from history. **DON'T TRUST A DEMON, Y'ALL.** Knowing that Peter wanted his aunt to live but could not make the tough call, Mary Jane stepped up to Mephisto and set the terms. She agreed to Mephisto's deal, but he would also never be allowed to come near Peter again. History was changed and Mary Jane and Peter were never married. Mary Jane saved the day and was arguably emotionally stronger than Peter.

Now free of her past strife, Mary Jane went back to being the vivacious and jubilant creature she had always been. She focused on her career. She opened two fabulous clubs, both of which were destroyed in Super Hero battles. (Can we say *not her fault* or what?!) After the closing of the second, Tony Stark approached Mary Jane about assisting him at **STARK INDUSTRIES**. Though it was difficult to again be a part of the Super Hero world, working for her ex's direct competition, Mary Jane thrived. She even had a brief escapade as a hero. She donned an **IRON SPIDER SUIT** to save both Peter and Tony, who were caught up in a losing battle. Though the costume life was not for her, she certainly remains a hero, and she does it with style.

NOT ALL HEROES HAVE SUPER-POWERS.

GAMORA

GAMORA IS FIERCE, fiery, and not in the mood for shenanigans—probably because she's the last of her kind. She is skilled with many weapons, but is best with her blade, **GODSLAYER**. Ya know, perfect for killing a mad god named Thanos. Gamora does NOT mess around. Although Gamora has had some passionate moments, feverish emotions are not what drive her in the slightest. Gamora is a sword-wielding, death-defying, space-traveling kind of gal. And though she's a bit of a lone wolf, she has also learned to open her heart and welcome a new chosen family, who are also pretty dang fierce themselves. Above all, Gamora is here to kick butts, take names, and **SAVE THE UNIVERSE**—not necessarily in that order. But she wasn't always a hero. Gamora started out on a villainous road that could have defined her, but instead she found her own path that allowed her to become the hero she was always meant to be.

GAMORA was born to a peaceful and devotedly religious alien race. Her upbringing was charmed and peaceful, until her people were obliterated by a competing evangelical religion. This religion was led by a purple jerk named the Magus. Gamora escaped, but she was orphaned and alone. Another purple jerk, the Mad Titan Thanos, rescued Gamora and raised the little girl. He also encouraged her lust for revenge. He could use her ire to exact vengeance on their mutual enemy—the Magus.

Being the murderous megalomaniac that he was, Thanos took Gamora pirating across the cosmos, developing her thirst for blood. He not only trained her in the deadly arts, but upgraded her body with bionic enhancements, making her the **DEADLIEST WOMAN IN THE GALAXY**. Let's be real here—Gamora was not exactly the best person during her early years. Thanos raised her as a living weapon, which meant that she spent a lot of time fighting for the wrong side. Even so, from the time that Gamora was a child, Thanos saw that there was too much good in her to make her truly capable of being the coldhearted assassin he was hoping to create. Gamora felt it, too. She was torn between pleasing her father and his cruel desires, and the softness she felt in her heart. Despite Thanos's cruelty, she loved her father and did his bidding.

Gamora and Thanos teamed up with another hero to help them conquer the Magus. His name was Adam Warlock and he was created to be genetically perfect—let's just say he was a pretty great guy, and Gamora noticed. Gamora had some major feels. But plot twist!

Squads: Guardians of the Galaxy
Nova Corps
Infinity Watch
Graces

Super-powers: Bionic enhancements
Precognitive tracking
Cosmic awareness

Skills: Martial arts
Weapons master
Skilled strategist
Acrobat
Very dry humor

Accessory: Godslayer

Ship: The *Milano*

Warlock was destined to become her mortal enemy, the Magus, in the future, because of time travel and different dimensions and that kind of stuff. It's complicated, so just roll with it. You can only imagine how torn Gamora was between stopping the Magus, feels for his younger self, and the complicated issues with her father, who wanted her future crush to die.

The new comrades defeated the Magus and all seemed well—until Gamora learned Thanos's true plot was not to save the universe from the Magus, but to rule it in his stead. He was just letting the Magus do the heavy lifting for him. Thanos planned to kill all of the stars, wiping out every lifeform on every planet that depended on those stars, as a sacrifice to his true love, the lady Death. Oh yes, did we mention Gamora's adoptive dad **IS IN LOVE WITH ACTUAL DEATH?!** Yeah, because that's a thing.

A switch went off in Gamora. Thanos had manipulated her anger to create a killing machine for his own devious purpose. She realized that her adoptive father's prejudices and maleficence had become her own,

but she did not have to follow in his footsteps. After all, we cannot help but learn what our parents teach us. They are the people who literally introduce us to the entire world or, in this case, galaxy. That said, we have the power to learn new lessons and choose who we want to become. Seeing the universe in a greater context and doing the right thing is what being a true hero is about. The greatest gift we can give ourselves is the chance to grow and become a better person, and that is exactly what Gamora did.

She went to warn her allies of Thanos's true intent, but before she could arrive she was attacked by Thanos's enemy Drax the Destroyer and was left wrecked. As she lay dying, her friend Adam Warlock found her and saved her soul inside his Infinity Stone—**THE SOUL GEM**. He was able to lock her essence within it until she could be resurrected. There she shared a heavenly space with her friend Pip the Troll, as well as others who were saved within the gem as a shared consciousness. This was basically a really nice all-inclusive vacation spot with a dash of existential crisis.

When Adam Warlock finally conquered Thanos, he took possession of the Mad Titan's all-powerful weapon, a bejeweled metal glove called the **INFINITY GAUNTLET**. Using its awesome power, he was able to bring Gamora and Pip back to life, though a piece of Gamora remained trapped within the gem. That's right—a part of her is literally missing.

Gamora, now freed, sought redemption and vengeance against the man who made her into a weapon—her adoptive father, Thanos. This new turn was not easy for Gamora. She continued to crave blood over diplomacy. Anger is hard to kill, though killing came easy. This probably would have been a great time to do some therapy and work on herself, but Gamora didn't have time for that. She had a galaxy full of adventures to explore.

She worked alongside Adam Warlock as part of his Infinity Watch to separate and protect the **INFINITY STONES** that powered Thanos's Infinity Gauntlet. She could not allow her father to ever again wield that kind of power over her or anyone else. However, Gamora relieved herself of duty after a falling-out with Adam.

She teamed up romantically and professionally with the super space cop **NOVA**, though they could not last because of her propensity for slicing bad guys up first and asking questions later. She was too much of an outlaw for this law-lover.

Gamora even trained a fellow green glamazon, She-Hulk, when she entered the **CONTEST OF CHAMPIONS**. They should probably be *best* friends, right? Green girls pumping iron all day!

But Gamora's most profound growth came from teaming up with her chosen space family: **THE GUARDIANS OF THE GALAXY**. Together, this motley crew of misfits saved the universe from time to time. They also caused some trouble, stole a few things, and lived in a moral gray area, which was the best place for a trained assassin to live. This band of unlikely heroes had an unexpected effect on Gamora. The closeness of the team began to break down her walls, and for the first time since she was orphaned, she had a family. But don't get me wrong, Gamora still thirsted endlessly for revenge against Thanos.

Gamora chased Thanos across the galaxy, sometimes even running from her teammates to exact revenge on Thanos for herself and her people. At one point, she even butted heads with Carol Danvers and the Guardians because they knew Thanos was on Earth and didn't tell her. Finally, the day came. She stood able to strike a killing blow against the man who harmed her, the man who made her kill. Her enemy. The only father she had ever known. This was the moment she had dreamed of for decades. However, something in Gamora had changed. It was all she'd ever wanted, and yet, there she was, unable to strike. She was better than that. Better than him. Capturing Thanos humanely was the only way to truly beat him and correct the lessons he had wrongfully instilled in her. Together with the help and encouragement of her

The Crew: Drax the Destroyer
Star-Lord
Rocket Raccoon
Groot

new heroic family, she captured Thanos and left him to spend the remainder of his days in prison. That should be plenty of time for reflection.

Gamora has a new family all her own, a real family. And sure, they are kind of smelly and one of them is a tree and another is a raccoon, but they are all hers. As friends and equals, they are there for each other, no matter what the galaxy brings.

Groot
I am Groot?

Gamora
Can you please give the communicator to Rocket?

Groot
I am Groot.

Gamora
How about Star-Lord?

Groot
I am GROOT.

Gamora
No. No one wants to talk to Drax.

win the hard way—

the right way—
not with hate,
not with retribution,
but with wisdom
and hope."

— KAMALA KHAN,
MS. MARVEL

MEDUSA

QUEEN. DIPLOMAT. HAIR RAISER.

GOD SAVE THE QUEEN! JK, this queen doesn't need to be saved. **MEDUSA** is the matriarch of a race of super-powered people called the **INHUMANS**. Her name might evoke the ancient Greek story of a woman with snakes swirling around her head, and that's for good reason. Medusa's hair is prehensile, enabling her long tresses to move like lengthy, formidable appendages. Yes, that means she can walk using her hair. She puts ladies in shampoo commercials to shame with her split-end-free, floor-length locks! Don't be too distracted by her fabulous hairdo, though—Medusa is a monarch who should inspire us all to lead with heart, eloquence, and intelligence.

But what are Inhumans?! They are a race of people from Earth that were genetically enhanced during the days of cavemen by aliens known as Kree. Now, when these seemingly normal humans are exposed to the Mist elicited from **TERRIGEN CRYSTALS**, they manifest fantastic gifts specific to each Inhuman. This is, of course, what gave Medusa her fierce hairstyle.

Medusa leads the Inhuman people alongside her husband, **BLACK BOLT**, the king, in the royal city of Attilan. Though the Inhumans live in a patriarchy, Medusa has much more power than you might assume a subservient female monarch to have. Because Black Bolt is gifted with a voice that can decimate a city (though much handier in a battle than a public address), Medusa has learned to understand Black Bolt without words. She serves as his translator and mouthpiece to present a unified front between the two of them. Sometimes she even bends his words to best suit her own message. It's easier to get the last word in when you're the only one who gets to talk, after all. Medusa's hair is powerful, but her words and her persuasiveness as a diplomat are arguably her greatest powers. Furthermore, the Inhuman people know *only* Medusa as the representative of their people, because her husband must stay silent. While Medusa speaks for all of Inhumanity and its king, she also rules as Black Bolt's equal.

A whole royal court surrounds Medusa, the first member of which is Medusa's younger sister, **CRYSTAL**, who can control the elements. Her brother-in-law is Maximus the Mad, a brilliant but treacherous usurper. His thirst for the crown, and his deceptive means of attaining it have long been a painful struggle for the royal family. Luckily, Medusa can lean on the bull-legged-stomping, earthquake-inducing **GORGON**, who serves as leader of the royal guard and is one of Medusa's dearest friends. Her cousins, the super calculating strategist Karnak and the fishy-faced Triton, round out her inner circle. Medusa and Black Bolt also have a child named Ahura, whose unstable Inhuman powers have caused him to be in and out of various care facilities, creating a point of tension for all of Attilan.

Super-power: Prehensile hair stronger than steel wire

Husband: Black Bolt

Skills: Hand-to-hair combat
Diplomacy

Oh, and I couldn't possibly forget the royal family's pet! **LOCKJAW**, the two-thousand-pound teleporting canine.

Because of King Black Bolt's profound need for Medusa to communicate with others, and because of the nature of their nonverbal communication, the love between the two of them is profound and intimate. Can you even imagine someone who can tell what you are thinking *all the time*? Secrets are few and far between when you can read every detail of someone's body language. However, when secrets they've kept from each other are revealed, the betrayal is unfathomable. Yeah, you can see where this is going. . . .

Black Bolt went behind Medusa's back and conspired with his brother Maximus the Mad to blow up Attilan with a Terrigen bomb. Sure, he was doing it to defeat an equally mad Titan named Thanos, and he evacuated most of his people, but the Inhuman city **ATTILAN** was destroyed, as was their entire supply of the super-power-giving substance Terrigen. Attilan fell into New York Harbor, and Black Bolt was assumed dead. Medusa's heart was broken and her people were strewn to the wind. She could not fall apart, though, because her people needed her. She became the sole leader of the Inhumans.

They needed to rebuild Attilan anew. And so they did—in the middle of the Hudson River. Being stuck in an unsanctioned city in the middle of a river wasn't ideal, but at least there was a good view of Manhattan, New Jersey, and the Statue of Liberty.

The last of the **TERRIGEN MISTS** spread over New York City and New Jersey. Many humans were killed by the intense vapors, while others cocooned and began their Inhuman transformation, unaware that they carried dormant Inhuman genes at all.

Though Medusa had seemingly lost her husband and her people were reeling, she knew she must continue to serve the Inhumans no matter the cost. Would-be usurpers like her brother-in-law Maximus the Mad think that being a ruler permits them to lord over and command others for their personal gain. That is, in fact, being a dictator. A true leader must serve those she leads. She is meant to teach, mentor, inspire, and pave the way through her own goodness, in addition to providing the structure in which her people will thrive. Knowing this, Medusa sought out her new Inhuman subjects being born from the Terrigen Mists released on Earth. These newly transformed people needed her. Though many did not understand how or why, they emerged forever changed from a chrysalis. Together with her fellow surviving Inhuman royals, Medusa brought together her new people and helped to guide them in their new lives.

The Terrigen Mists did much more than create new Inhumans. In fact, they probably should've come with a warning. Something like "Side effects may include death." The mists killed a lot of people on Earth and left others injured or adversely affected. Medusa had to make the

Fun Fact: The Inhuman city of Attilan has existed in many places, from the Himalayas to outer space, on the dark side of the moon, and a host of places in between. Now New Attilan lives in the Hudson River.

difficult decision to rid the Earth of the vapors entirely, though it also meant she would not be able to create any future Inhumans. The entire supply of Terrigen would be eliminated. Nobody carrying an Inhuman gene would ever be able to transform into their super-powered state again. Despite the crippling effect it would have on the lineage of Inhumans, Medusa knew she must make the decision to save the greatest number of people. Heavy is the head that wears the crown—or the very long hair. However you want to look at it.

Black Bolt resurfaced, totally alive, but his relationship with Medusa could never be the same. He had betrayed her and their people, leaving her to pick up the pieces. Furthermore, they'd both grown and changed during their time apart. They no longer were the people they were when they were younger. They chose to separate as lovers, but remained partners. They could still love and co-parent their son, **AHURA**, serve their people, and maintain a deep and meaningful friendship. Love takes all kinds of forms, and sometimes a relationship matures to a place where two people can love each other without being *in* love with each other.

Together with the royal family, Medusa searched through outer space and found a new source of Terrigen, a purer form called **PRIMAGEN**, and with it, the promise of future Inhumans was restored. Medusa remains queen of the Inhumans, promising to serve her people in any situation, no matter how hairy.

GHOST-SPIDER

SPIDER-GWEN. SPIDER-WOMAN. SPIDER-ROCK-STAR.

WITH GREAT POWER comes great responsibility, and even more band practice. The **GWEN STACY** of the main Marvel Universe, Earth-616, may have died in the arms of Peter Parker, but in the dimension of Earth-65 it was Gwen Stacy who lived and Peter who died. Now Gwen lives as the costumed vigilante **GHOST-SPIDER**, chasing down villains as small as the Bodega Bandit all the way up to the Kingpin named Matt Murdock (who was the hero Daredevil on Earth-616, but is a sly devil on Earth-65).

> Oh hey, this is a good time to explain some stuff about Earth-65. Gwen's home dimension is a lot like the Marvel Universe that we know and love, but in this world some heroes are villains and some people who are alive in one dimension are dead in this one, and sometimes a guy is a girl, etc. Basically, you can't assume that people from our universe are like their Earth-65 counterparts, other than the occasional physical similarities. Phew! Glad we cleared that up!

So back to Gwen. She truly rocks, and not just because she is a fierce drummer for her band, the Mary Janes. She's a devoted friend and daughter. And honestly, she's just trying to figure out all this Super Hero stuff and keep her after-school job selling hot dogs before the place is smashed up again by some dang Super Villain. Gwen Stacy is proof positive that you can try to do the right thing and it can still come out wrong. But hey, you have to keep trying either way!

Let's start at the beginning. Gwen Stacy was bitten by a genetically modified spider while at a science demonstration about radioactivity. The bite gave her **SPIDEY-SENSES** to predict danger, the ability to cling to walls with her fingers and toes, and the proportional speed and strength of a spider. Gwen spent her time out of costume working hard in high school, hanging with her besties, Peter Parker and Harry Osborn, and crushing the drums in the Mary Janes.

However, her secret exploits as **SPIDER-WOMAN** made Peter Parker desperate to follow in her web-prints. Especially after Gwen saved him from bullies in a humiliating display. She was trying to help her friend, but it only made things worse for him. Using a chemical power-up by Midtown High teacher Dr. Connors, Peter hoped to transform himself into someone extraordinary like Spider-Woman. Instead he turned himself into a giant rampaging Lizard, who ruined prom. Gwen had to save the innocent bystanders, so she began fighting the

Name: Gwen Stacy

Aliases: Ghost-Spider
Spider-Gwen
Spider-Woman
Gwennie

Skills: Hand-to-hand combat
Drumming
Fast food service

Super-powers: Spidey-senses
Wall-crawling
Super-speed
Super-strength

Band: The Mary Janes

Father: Captain George Stacy

Least-Threatening Nemesis: Bodega Bandit and his dog Bandito

Most-Threatening Nemesis: The Kingpin Matt Murdock

Spider-Bae: Spider-Man from Earth-616, aka Miles Morales

Determined to make amends for unwittingly killing her best friend, Peter, Gwen spent her free time swinging around NYC taking down criminals and trying to prove herself a hero.

During one of her heroic encounters, she stepped in to **SAVE HER FATHER** from a hit man. Captain Stacy took this as an opportunity to turn on her, despite the fact that she saved his flippin' life! In a moment of vulnerability, she revealed her secret identity to her father. Her only hope of escape was her father's love. Captain Stacy let her go, but now he had a much bigger problem: clearing his daughter's name, even though doing so meant technically aiding and abetting a criminal.

Her father was there for her when she needed him most. Confiding in a parent sometimes seems hard, but they've lived a lot more life and sometimes they understand more than their kids think they will. Sure, Captain Stacy wasn't ever a Super Hero, but he did know what it meant to serve and protect. He knew that people make mistakes because he had made mistakes. Allowing her father to see behind the mask gave Gwen another person in her corner and a promise that she did not have to face the challenges of heroism alone.

In the midst of all this, Gwen was called away to help Peter Parker of the main Marvel Universe, **EARTH-616**, defeat a bunch of dimension-hopping "Inheritors" that liked to eat spider-people. Gross! On the bright side, coming together with so many spider-people gave Gwen exactly what she needed—**A SUPPORT SYSTEM AND MENTORSHIP.**

Learning that there was *another* Gwen Stacy who died in *another* dimension made it hard for Gwen not to be curious about what could have been her fate. Jessica Drew, Earth-616's Spider-Woman, was kind enough to remind Gwen that you just can't compare yourself to others, no matter how similar they might seem. There is only one you, and only you can do your life. It's like Theodore Roosevelt said: "Comparison is the thief of joy."

crazed Lizard. How could she know it was actually her best friend, Peter?! Transforming back to his human form, Peter Parker died from his injuries in Gwen's arms. Tragic much?

Now considered a murderer, Spider-Woman was on the run, hunted by the entire police force. To make matters worse, her own father, **CAPTAIN GEORGE STACY**, was leading the investigative charge in true witch-hunt fashion. And as if that weren't enough, she was also lambasted by the press, thanks to the diligent muckraking of editor-in-creep J. Jonah Jameson.

Gwen's BFF, Harry Osborn, left to join the army and become an Agent of S.H.I.E.L.D. And her girl crew, the Mary Janes, were increasingly torn apart by Gwen's depression and absence.

Spider-Gwen

Swinging by the bodega. Need anything?

Spider-Man Peter

Coffee, please. Thanks, kid.

Spider-Woman Jess

I'll take anything with bacon!

Spider-Ham

. . . WOW.

Spider-Gwen

. . . maybe I just get coffees for everybody.

There is no manual for how to be a hero, or even for how to grow up to be a decent person. Luckily, Gwen could lean on another Spider-Woman. Well, not *literally*, because Jessica was VERY pregnant at the time—but she still had plenty of good advice. When in doubt, a mentor who has followed a similar path or has similar interests, or, in this case, has super-powers, can be an important step in anyone's growth. Spider-Woman took Gwen on patrol, and offered advice, which was sometimes more about snacks than punching bad guys (pregnancy makes you hungry) but still helpful.

Perhaps things would've turned out better if Gwen had taken more of Jessica's advice, because things weren't going great. Her old BFF, Harry Osborn, returned as a chemical-fueled rage monster. **THE MARY JANES** teetered on the edge of abject failure, and her bandmates became increasingly aware of Gwen's notable *absences* during Spider-Woman's notable *appearances*. Oh, and

Gwen's father landed himself in jail after admitting his association with Spider-Woman.

Gwen knew that her father's only hope for staying out of jail was to go through Kingpin Matt Murdock, who was also the district attorney and didn't mind making a crooked deal. So in a moment of weakness, she agreed to work for the Kingpin. It had seemed like the best option at the time, even if it was making a deal with the devil. The only downside was that he also happened to be a mob boss and leader to a boatload of ninja assassins. But ya know, **HINDSIGHT IS 20/20**.

It was important for Gwen to have at least one peer she could talk to, even if he did live in another dimension. So, when **MILES MORALES** hopped into Earth-65 looking for his father, he and Gwen had an instant connection. Spider-powers, tragedies, daddy issues, homework—what *didn't* they have in common? Though a long-distance relationship didn't make sense between dimensions, the two promised to stay friends. Didn't stop them from smooching anyway. . . .

Now she must face the Kingpin, save her father, and protect all of New York City. That's a lot of work for one girl, but she is up to the task. She is still learning how to be a good Super Hero, and how to be a good person, too. She is making mistakes along the way, but with a little help from her friends, she's well on her way to being the best Gwen Stacy that she can be.

VALKYRIE

SHIELD-MAIDEN. ASGARDIAN. FEARLESS DEFENDER.

VALKYRIE is the leader of the Valkyrior, a horde of Asgardian warrior demigoddesses working for the big guy in the Norse sky, Odin. Basically, these gals are **BUTT-KICKING ANGELS**. Their chief duty is to deliver the worthy dead from their battlefields to the heavenly realm of **VALHALLA**—sometimes even intervening during combat to help their warriors win the day. These brawling babes are the most formidable warriors in the heavens. The most notable of these fierce women is **BRUNNHILDE**, the head of the shield-maidens.

Brunnhilde has spent most of her godly life overseeing warriors in battle and sometimes protecting them through her own intervention. Like many Asgardians, she has shared bodies with Earthly humans—such as activist Samantha Parrington, cultist Barbara Norriss, and archaeologist Annabelle Riggs—but she still remains the one true Valkyrie.

Imagine a time long, long ago, when the small kingdoms of Europe still existed in citadels, roads were made of dirt, and the people enjoyed watching sword fights like they were at Medieval Times—because it was in fact medieval times. In the ancient land of **WRLSTEAD ARMS**, Valkyrie was a princess. Not the kind who wears fancy dresses and drinks tea, but the kind who studies how to wield a broadsword, rocks a metal bra, and thirsts only for victory at the side of her brawny beau, the master of arms, Sigmund.

Odin came down to Midgard (Earth in Asgardian speak), spreading war across Europe. He stormed the Wrlstead Arms castle, but Brunnhilde would not hide. Instead, the headstrong young woman went in search of her father, the king, who she prayed was safe. Sigmund tried to protect her in the fray, but took an arrow while shielding her. As Sigmund lay dying in Brunnhilde's arms, Valkyrie's only concern was her ailing love. The opposing troops marched toward her, but she was fearless. She was too overcome with grief, too furious to care about anything else. Odin himself offered her mercy so that she might escape his army. But Brunnhilde did not want his pity. She stood up to the king of the gods with fire and determination. Can you even imagine?! **SHE SAID NO TO ODIN HIMSELF**. She didn't need his pity! She refused to leave Sigmund's body behind.

Seeing her steadfast spirit and devotion to her dead warrior, Odin recognized something special in her. He offered her a godly position as his personal Valkyrie. As Valkyrie, she would deliver his true believers and worthy warriors from battle to the heavenly realm of Valhalla to stand by his side. As a reward, she could one day join Sigmund in Valhalla to live in eternal bliss. With ferocity and love in her heart, Brunnhilde accepted his offer so

---

Name: Brunnhilde

Alias: Valkyrie

Human Hosts: Samantha Parrington, Barbara Norriss, Annabelle Riggs

Skills: Fierce warrior
Allspeak
Accomplished Pegasus rider

Super-powers: Godly strength, speed, and agility
Nearly immortal healing
Can perceive impending death
Teleportation

that men like her dear Sigmund could enjoy a heavenly afterlife.

Hello! How fearless is that?! To resign yourself to carrying heroes into the afterlife?! **TO DEFY A GOD?!** Valkyrie plays by her own rules.

Valkyrie stood up for herself and what she believed in, and was rewarded. She took control of her own destiny, which positioned her to become a leader. This rebel spirit would come to inform her work as a goddess and commander for years to come.

As the leader of her fellow **VALKYRIOR**, Brunnhilde was charged with serving Odin, but sometimes she was guided by her own sense of righteousness and compassion. In fact, Valkyrie once defied Odin's decree in order to save a warrior she felt was worthier than his sadistic opponent. Odin himself stepped in to kill her champion (for no one could disobey the command of Odin as king of the gods or whatever, **BLAH, BLAH, PATRIARCHY**). Valkyrie was to be punished for disobeying him. What was Valkyrie's punishment, you ask? To be sent to Midgard and live a mortal life in which she would have to be subservient to her husband—for she was to fall in love with the first man she set eyes on. This was literally Valkyrie's worst nightmare. Not just mortality, but to be tied to someone undeserving of her and to lead an ordinary life.

VALKYRIE LIVES FOR HER FREEDOM! She rides on the wind and thrives in the space between life and death. Valkyrie would rather bear bloodied bodies to Valhalla than be with a man who did not deserve her. Let. That. Sink. In. We might all value our freedom and bliss over the confines of attachment as Valkyrie does. Love is indeed a rare gift, but to be tied down for the sake of it is hardly a treat. Valkyrie instead finds fulfillment in her

Valkyrie Checklist: Metal bra
Huge sword
Pegasus
Ye Olde Speake
Bangin' braids

Base: The heavenly realm of Valhalla, the golden Asgardian city inhabited by the worthy dead

work and closeness in her relationships with her fellow bad baes—the Valkyrior. Her life is full and exhilarating. Though her punishment was rescinded, it would not be the last time Valkyrie caused troubles for the king of the gods or that her freedom was put in peril.

The Bifrost, also known as the Rainbow Bridge, is the only permanent portal to Midgard from Asgard. After the events of Ragnarok, the Bifrost was destroyed, shattering any connection between the two realms. Without the passageway, Valkyrie became tired of the heavens. Gods don't really die all that often, so it was pretty boring. She was enticed by the beguiling goddess Amora the Enchantress with the promise of adventure outside Valhalla's walls. How could our wild Valkyrie refuse? We must choose our friends carefully, especially those who lure us with tempting promises. Promises that seem to be too good to be true. Valkyrie soon saw that her strength was being misused for the Enchantress's own deceitful gain. Valkyrie stood up to the bewitching goddess, but Amora was unwilling to surrender Valkyrie's impressive muscle. Instead the Enchantress imprisoned Valkyrie's soul within her blade.

The Enchantress used Valkyrie as her weapon against the heroes of Midgard, taking revenge on men who spurned her. She forced Valkyrie to possess the bodies of humans on Midgard and wreak havoc in their place. Under the control of the Enchantress, Valkyrie first took over the body of a well-to-do socialite and women's equality activist, Samantha Parrington. Valkyrie used Samantha's passion for equal rights and public visibility as a socialite as a way to lash out at men under the villainous trance of the Enchantress. Though Valkyrie was a powerful woman, she did not wish to spurn men for the sake of it. That was the misguided desire of the Enchantress coursing through poor Valkyrie's musclebound body. Later, a cultist named Barbara Norriss saw the errors of her ways and sacrificed herself to save Doctor Strange and the Hulk. **THE DEFENDERS** later rescued Barbara from the dimension she had been trapped in, but she had been driven

mad by the experience. The Defenders imprisoned her along with Amora the Enchantress. Finally, being in the presence of another woman, Amora knew how to break free! She called Valkyrie into Barbara's body. Valkyrie freed Amora, but realized she would be better suited to serve the Defenders as a hero rather than serving the untrustworthy goddess. Valkyrie became a Defender, and they helped Valkyrie free herself from Amora's imprisonment and inhabit her own Asgardian body once and for all.

Misty Knight
Hey, hon, what are you up to?

Valkyrie
I stand in battle against the dark elves.

Misty Knight
I'll Val-hollah at you later then. ;)

Valkyrie
Are you to die in battle?

Misty Knight
. . . I hope not.

Valkyrie
'Tis my regret.

Misty Knight
I'm glad we're friends, but can you stop hoping for me to die?

Valkyrie is now able to finally live the free and fabulous life she always dreamed of. She has fought alongside **THE DEFENDERS**, **THE SECRET AVENGERS**, and was even recruited by a group of interdimensional **EXILES** to protect the multiverse from the reality-devouring Time-Eater. Calling on her signature zeal for life, war, and horses, she slashes her way through the many dimensions with Blink, Iron Lad, Khan, and the adorable Wolvie in the hopes of making all the realms of the heavens and Midgard a better place for all people.

MONICA RAMBEAU

POWERHOUSE. ELECTRIC PERSONALITY. BRIGHT.

MONICA RAMBEAU is a pioneering woman in the Marvel Universe. This woman is powerful! She is a leader, a force to be reckoned with, oh, and she's made up of **PURE ENERGY** from the electromagnetic spectrum. She broke the mold as a lieutenant in the New Orleans Harbor Patrol, and as the **FIRST AFRICAN AMERICAN WOMAN** Super Hero to join the Avengers. She even went on to become the Avengers' official chairperson. Heck yes! That's right—she was one of the few women to *lead* the Avengers!

What makes her such an amazing leader? Monica isn't just an insanely powerful Super Hero with all of the **FORCES OF LIGHT AND ENERGY** behind her; she's also never afraid to question the status quo and shut down bad behavior. She stood up to Iron Man, letting him know in no uncertain terms her name isn't "babe." She'll call out sexism in a snap, because sometimes people need to know that even well-intentioned behavior can be entirely uncool. Monica doesn't tolerate bad behavior, even from the good guys, and especially not from the bad ones. Furthermore, she puts the needs of others before herself, because above all, Monica is here to serve and protect.

Monica Rambeau was part of the New Orleans Harbor Patrol, where she dreamed of climbing to the rank of captain, but her boss had no intention of promoting her to such heights. Monica was an outspoken live wire who played by her own rules, and on top of all that, she was a woman of color. Passed over again and again for promotions, Monica was furious and frustrated. So, when she was asked for help by her grandfather's old work associate, Professor Andre LeClare, she figured she didn't have much to lose. He was in deep trouble because his research into interdimensional energies was taken by his old assistant in hopes of weaponizing it. The energy and technology was incredibly volatile, not to mention it had the potential to rip a hole between dimensions.

Together, LeClare and Rambeau took her patrol boat to find the assistant on an old Roxxon oil rig out in the ocean. Posing as a sexy sunbather, she convinced the

---

Name: Monica Rambeau

Aliases: Captain Marvel, Pulsar, Photon, Spectrum

Hometown: New Orleans, LA

Super-powers: Transforms into energy
Flight
Moves at speed of light
Energy blasts
Intangibility
Cosmic awareness

Skills: Boat driver
Combatant
Detective leader

Brightness Meter: 11 out of 10 sunglasses

Ultimate Power Couple: The semi-silver fox Adam Brashear, aka the Blue Marvel, possesses similar energy absorption powers

Squads: Avengers, Mighty Avengers, Ultimates

sailors to let her board the ship to enjoy the view. However, when LeClare got impatient and decided to stow away to find the machine, he blew her cover. In a last-ditch effort to dismantle the dangerous machine, Monica punched into its circuits. Something strange took place. A flash of light coursed through her body as she absorbed **INTERDIMENSIONAL ENERGIES**. In an instant, she was turned into pure electromagnetic energy! Suddenly able to fly, she headed back to the mainland at the speed of light. Confused, she found herself in a warehouse full of Mardi Gras costumes. She grabbed her classic white outfit to cover her swimsuit and flew back to the rig. (Convenient way to get a Super

Hero costume, eh?) There, she saved LeClare, closed a strange, growing portal between dimensions, called in the Navy to help shut down Roxxon's rig, and saved the day! The men of the ship called her both *Captain* and a marvel, so she took it as her first Super Hero name: **CAPTAIN MARVEL**. If people think you're marvelous, you have to own it. And own it she did.

Not long after Monica's transformation into a being composed of interdimensional energies, she had a chance encounter with Spider-Man in NYC that introduced her to the Avengers. She needed to channel her literal energies or she might cause an explosion! The Avengers helped her to disperse her energies. Seeing

Monica's clear potential, they invited her to stick around for training. After only a few weeks, the Avengers' leader, Janet Van Dyne (aka the Wasp), asked her to join the team, making her the first African American woman to become one of Earth's Mightiest Heroes.

Monica Rambeau took the name of Captain Marvel, not knowing it belonged to a recently deceased Super Hero named Captain Mar-Vell. (Awkward!) Her fellow heroes initially encouraged her to keep the name, because her immense ability was considered an honor to the fallen hero. However, the son of Captain Mar-Vell, Genis-Vell, came back to Earth using his father's old name. Monica gracefully agreed to take the name **PHOTON** instead. But when Genis-Vell abandoned the name, he then took on the name Photon. *Say what?!* He managed to take her name twice! Monica had to again change her alias, but this time the two hashed it out over a coffee and decided she'd take the name **PULSAR**. Later she would embrace her full colors under the name **SPECTRUM**. But let's just call her **MONICA RAMBEAU**. She does have a real spectrum of names, though.

Only a few weeks later, the Wasp stepped down as chairwoman of the Avengers for a little rest and relaxation. As you can imagine, leading the team was a lot of work. Captain America himself nominated Monica Rambeau for the role of chairwoman. At first, Monica was reluctant to accept; she was new to the team, after all. Thor immediately jumped in, questioning Monica's capability, and offered himself instead, but She-Hulk quickly interceded. She-Hulk slowed everyone down, and with her vote of confidence gave Monica an opportunity to actually accept. Women in leadership need each other's support, and this was truly a beautiful moment of **ENCOURAGEMENT AND SISTERHOOD** among Avengers.

It is important to encourage our friends to fulfill their potential. In today's world, women are still overlooked for leadership positions, and sometimes ladies themselves doubt their own abilities because of unspoken societal constructs. The only way for women to grow into leadership roles is to **LIFT EACH OTHER UP** by cheering on capable ladies with diverse voices and gifts. Like Monica, you may not realize that you're the leader a team needs until someone brings it to your attention! It's never too late to take a stand as a leader in your community.

Emboldened by She-Hulk's words and Captain America's nomination, Monica accepted. Monica was the first **WOMAN OF COLOR** to lead Earth's Mightiest Heroes.

Monica led the Avengers against a serious gallery of rogues, including actual gods. But an encounter with a sea monster named Leviathan left Monica stretched thin. She had literally spread her energy so greatly that it left her depleted and nearly depowered. Monica was in bad shape. Her parents took her home to convalesce and eat some delicious home cooking. Monica had to step away from the Avengers to heal, but when she was back on her feet she would be ready to again answer the call. Monica was far from finished leading the hero team, though. It was only the beginning.

Monica was a born leader and returned to the helm of **THE MIGHTY AVENGERS** alongside the man with unbreakable skin, Luke Cage, magical martial artist White Tiger, the insanely powerful Blue Marvel, and others. She also joined the **ULTIMATES** alongside the king of Wakanda, Black Panther, the teen titan America Chavez, and Captain Marvel (Carol Danvers this time).

On some teams Monica led, on others she followed. But on all of her teams, Monica remains a beacon of integrity. Her wise words are matched only by her veracity and dedication. Not to mention, her body is made of pure energy—so she continues to be literally powerful. And maybe her Super Hero names never really stuck, but what's in a name, anyway? Monica Rambeau by any other name is still one of the most powerful people on Earth.

TERRIFIC TWOSOMES

FIGHTING CRIME and saving the day is always more fun with a friend by your side! These fearless friends offer each other endless support, good laughs, work opportunities, real talk, and of course, a power-up on the battlefield.

Butt-Kicking Besties

CAPTAIN MARVEL & SPIDER-WOMAN

Captain Marvel and Spider-Woman are total **#GOALS**. These ladies know what it's like being a Super Hero day in and day out, and always know they can support each other. Sometimes being an **AVENGER** is a lot to handle, and no one understands that better than a fellow Avenger. Plus, it's always good to have a lady friend to talk to when Avengers Mansion is full of sweaty menfolk. Even when these ladies disagree, they manage to encourage each other and find common ground—which usually involves bacon.

HAWKEYE & AMERICA

Kate Bishop and America Chavez first teamed up with **THE YOUNG AVENGERS**, with whom they cemented their reputation as **ULTIMATE BFFS**. And not just because they are the team's notable ladies, but also because they have the sassiest comebacks. These freewheeling young women enjoy a good road trip, an impromptu slumber party, sharing life advice, leaning on each other, and punching up baddies. Now that America is in an alternate-dimension college and Kate has moved to Venice Beach, the girls don't get as much in-person time, so it's a good thing they have an out-of-this-world data plan.

SHE-HULK & HELLCAT

These straight-talkin' gal pals have been through it all! **JENNIFER WALTERS** (aka She-Hulk), employed her bestie, **PATSY WALKER** (aka Hellcat), as a private detective for her law firm, and Patsy has employed Jennifer as her lawyer. Their friendship is hardly all business, though. They share a bevy of their civilian pals and quality time together. They love to hit the club together, grab brunch with a group of fab friends, or just visit a taco truck or two. And of course, they are always around to help battle each other's awful exes and online dates.

Power Couples

ANGELA & SERA

Angela and Sera are angels from the tenth realm of **HEVEN!** Together these battle-ready seraphim have literally been to Hel and back for each other. When Sera was imprisoned in the afterlife, Angela overthrew **HELA**, the goddess of death, so that she might return Sera to the realm of the living. That is love! Now they can enjoy cuddling on their couch together in heavenly peace.

CLOAK & DAGGER

You cannot have light without dark, or Cloak without Dagger. After meeting as runaways, **TANDY BOWEN** and **TYRONE JOHNSON** were abducted and experimented on. Now Tandy (aka Dagger) is able to channel energy to create **PSIONIC LIGHT DAGGERS**, while Cloak can produce **A PORTAL TO THE DARKFORCE DIMENSION**, allowing him to teleport and channel dark energy. Their complementary powers of dark and light are symbiotically balanced so neither is overtaken by the light or dark inside themselves. They also share a deep affection for each other that is only intensified by the intimacy and necessity of each other's powers.

Sister Sister

MEDUSA AND CRYSTAL

Royal sisterhood has never been so hairy! Medusa, the prehensile-maned queen of the **INHUMANS**, and her younger, element-controlling sister, Crystal, would do anything for each other. Though Terrigen, Super Villains, and complex romantic relationships have threatened their sisterly bond, these women have managed to remain close. They also work together not just as Super Heroes, but as royals. Crystal serves as an Inhuman diplomat reporting to Medusa in order to protect the interests of **NEW ATTILAN** and Inhumans everywhere.

GAMORA & NEBULA

These sisters don't share blood (unless you count *bad* blood), but they do share the worst adoptive dad in the universe, Thanos! Both girls were taken in by the genocidal maniac to be raised as living weapons. They were pitted against each other in a lethal sibling rivalry. Because of her superior fighting prowess, Gamora was deemed the deadliest woman in the galaxy. The competition left Nebula bitter and power hungry. Over the years and through numerous battles, against each other and their father, Gamora and Nebula have learned that they no longer have to fight their father's battles, or each other. In fact, they actually might be on the **SAME SIDE**. Despite everything they've been through, there is still a lot of **SISTERLY LOVE**.

SQUIRREL GIRL

EATS NUTS. KICKS BUTTS.

DOREEN GREEN isn't just your average computer science major, she's one of the most **POWERFUL** characters in the Marvel Universe. No, really! She possesses all the super abilities of both a squirrel and a girl. Which means she can talk to squirrels, use her fluffy prehensile tail like a weapon, wallop with **SQUIRREL-LIKE STRENGTH** (which is surprisingly strong at human-size ratio), slice with razor-sharp nails, and, of course, hold all the majestic powers one possesses as a girl. Though she might seem cute and fluffy, don't scoff! Squirrel Girl has taken down some of Marvel's biggest baddies, from Thanos to a planet-size world eater. Though she *does* often rely on her head and heart instead of her fists and a horde of adorable rodents to win the day. (You really haven't seen a good fight until you've seen a Super Villain engulfed in squirrels, trust me.)

While Squirrel Girl's rodent powers are incredible, her compassion and warmth are what make her an acorn in the rough. Though villains may appear battle-ready, there's usually a greater issue behind their evildoing—and it usually doesn't have to do with a desire to fight. Everyone is the hero of their own story—even evil geniuses and big palookas who smash up banks. Everyone has dreams, wants, and needs. Before Squirrel Girl gets out her scratchy claws to fight, she asks herself and sometimes her foe, "Why are they doing this? Do they need money? Friendship? A good snack? How can I help this person without anyone getting hurt?" You can win a fight by defusing it and (BONUS) you make unlikely friends! And who doesn't want more friends?!

Growing up in Los Angeles, Doreen initially hid her powers to avoid embarrassment. But she found solace in her squirrel friend **MONKEY JOE**—who was not a monkey, just a squirrel. After Doreen saved him from a dog, he encouraged her to become a Super Hero. She had a natural gift! She caught up with Iron Man, hoping to finally prove herself and impress him enough to earn an invitation to be his sidekick. Though she totally saved Iron Man and conquered the attacking Super Villain (Yes! She saved Iron Man on her first time out of the flippin' gate!), he still refused her generous offer. She also helped the Hulk to beat up a big mutated beast named Abomination, but he offered her little credit and didn't really seem to be the "playing well with others" type. Squirrel Girl would not give up on her dreams so easily, though. Maybe she needed to be a hero all on her own.

Squirrel Girl set off for New York City—the home of Super Heroes! She didn't hit the big time right away, but she did protect Central Park and its squirrels from

Name: Doreen Allene Green		**Bases:**	NYC, Empire State University, GLA HQ under Lake Michigan
Alias: Squirrel Girl			
Nuts-for-Hugs-o-Meter: 12 out of 10		**Super-powers:**	All the powers of a squirrel All the powers of a girl
Squads: New Avengers, Great Lakes Avengers, US Avengers		**Skills:**	Chitter (squirrel talk) Computer science Creative problem-solving

Super-Villainous threats. It was there that she was scouted by the **GREAT LAKES AVENGERS**. (She was kind enough to save them from muggers, so they knew she was the real deal.)

For several years, she worked with them to protect the Midwest, this alliance later being known as the Great Lakes Defenders and Great Lakes Champions. Finding your **PERSONAL BRAND** and a catchy name can be hard—especially when the Avengers send you a cease-and-desist letter. Doreen would eventually make her way back to New York to work for the New Avengers, aka

become the nanny to Jessica Jones and Luke Cage's daughter, Danielle Cage.

Deciding to pursue higher education, Doreen enrolled at Empire State University to study computer science. She was assigned a dorm and a roommate, Nancy Whitehead. Though both girls hit it off, Doreen's best squirrel friend, **TIPPY-TOE**, was not too pleased with Nancy's cat, Mew, but they made it work. Doreen was quick to expand her hero circle as well. ESU had plenty of folks to team up with, including the dreamy **CHIPMUNK HUNK** and the unsinkable **KOI BOI**, who wasn't afraid of a little fish-to-cuffs. It's not your average team of Super Heroes, but Doreen is hardly average. She balances her time in classes with taking on some of the biggest and strangest villains in the universe. Luckily, her new team has helped Doreen to be not only a better Super Hero, but a more thoughtful one.

In fact, when Doreen's new super crew encountered the Hydra-programmed cyborg **BRAIN DRAIN**, Doreen and her fellow animal-themed heroes pounced on him without pause. Realizing that they hadn't even given him a chance to be friendly, Doreen made amends. Not only did they patch the hero up, but they used their computer science knowledge from school to update his operating

Parents: Maureen Green and Dorian Green

Mentor: Tony Stark

BFFs: Tippy-Toe
- Squirrel sidekick
- Nuts for nuts
- #TreeLyfe

Nancy Whitehead
- Doreen's roommate
- Knitting enthusiast
- Has a cat named Mew

Chipmunk Hunk, aka Tomas Lara-Perez
- Handsome puncher of bad guys
- All the powers of a chipmunk and a hunk

Koi Boi, aka Ken Shiga
- Unsinkable swimmer
- Speaks to fish and people
- Tips the scales of justice

Brain Drain, aka Brian Drayne
- Reprogrammed cyborg
- Hat person
- Existentialist poet

College: Empire State University
(Spider-Man went there!)

Major: Computer Science

Coolest Mode of Transport: The Squirrel-a-gig

HOW TO HIDE A TAIL
1. Put on yoga pants
2. Fold tail into the shape of a bodacious behind
3. Rock yoga pants so hard

systems and delete the Hydra propaganda making him a grade-A jerk. Brain Drain was reformed into the friendly scarf-and-hat-donning Brian Drayne: ESU student and **GENERALLY WEIRD BFF**.

Her first encounter with Brain Drain taught Squirrel Girl a valuable lesson: that she cannot be the one to strike first. She not only recognized her mistake, but admitted it and took actions to make amends. We all slip up, especially in the heat of the moment, but if we pause and take a moment to think, we can often course-correct. Because Doreen took a moment to realize that she was potentially in the wrong, she completely turned around someone else's life! She was able to reach out to him, and make a new friend. Sure, he's a pretty weird friend, but he's a friend nonetheless!

Squirrel Girl **CONTINUES TO GROW** as a student of computer science and of Super Hero-ing, but she still has a lot to learn. Luckily, she can lean on her mentor, Tony Stark, and her heroic friends. Oh, and Tippy-Toe. She's small, but sturdy.

Tony Stark @starkmantony
@unbeatablesg I am not making any more armor!

Squirrel Girl! @unbeatablesg
@starkmantony Hear me out

Tony Stark @starkmantony
@unbeatablesg No

Squirrel Girl! @unbeatablesg
@starkmantony A flight suit for Tippy-Toe

Tony Stark @starkmantony
@unbeatablesg No

Squirrel Girl! @unbeatablesg
@starkmantony No need to build a new one! @Antman will shrink an old one for you, right Scott?

Scott Lang @Antman
@unbeatablesg @starkmantony Sure, but it'll cost you $50

Tony Stark @starkmantony
@Antman @unbeatablesg I am not going to shrink an Iron Man armor for your squirrel friend

Scott Lang @Antman
@starkmantony @unbeatablesg Does that mean I'm not getting 50 bucks?

Squirrel Girl! @unbeatablesg
@Antman @starkmantony How about $50 and you make Tippy-Toe ENORMOUS!!!

Scott Lang @Antman
@unbeatablesg @starkmantony Sure!!

Tony Stark @starkmantony
@Antman @unbeatablesg Ugh, everyone. NO! NO GIANT SQUIRRELS

Squirrel Girl! @unbeatablesg
@starkmantony Does that mean you'll give Tippy-Toe a flight suit?!?!

Squirrel Girl! @unbeatablesg
@starkmantony? Hello?

Squirrel Girl! @unbeatablesg
@starkmantony I'm going to take the silence as a resounding YES!

MANTIS

MANTIS might seem like a delicate flower, but don't be fooled by her Zen demeanor. The likes of Mantis have rarely been seen anywhere in the universe. She is a master martial artist able to drop dudes twice her size, a telepath, and was chosen by an alien race as the perfect human being. Her powers are immense in every way imaginable! She also has learned a great deal from her strange life. Oh, and did I mention that she's an **AVENGER** *and a* **GUARDIAN OF THE GALAXY**?

Mantis was born in Vietnam to a German mercenary father and a Vietnamese mother. Her mother's brother Kruul was king of the Saigon underworld, and did not approve of the union between his sister and a foreigner. With Kruul aiming to kill them both, the young lovers were forced to go on the run. Ten months later, Mantis was born. Unfortunately, Kruul caught up with them. In a devastating explosion, her mother lost her life and her father lost his vision. Mantis and her father were taken in by the Priests of Pama at a local temple. Not only was she raised in the temple, but she and her father were trained in the martial arts there as well. Unbeknownst to either of them, the priests were actually an alien colony of **KREE** and **COTATI** pacifists. The Kree passed for humans, while the Cotati, who bore telepathic roots, passed as trees. Being raised under the Kree gave Mantis unbelievable fighting skills, and being raised around the telepathic Cotati imbued her with **EMPATHIC POWERS** that allowed her to feel and affect people's emotions, as well as communicate psychically.

Mantis' empathy has set her apart from every hero of her time. Not only can she sense people's emotions—she can truly experience what they feel. This is a super-power that even we simple humans can explore. If we focus on how another person might feel, we can begin to empathize with their experience. In our minds, we can explore things they've shared with us and imagine how those experiences might be shaping their thought process, body, or emotional state. We may not have Mantis' psychic abilities to help us *truly* know how someone else feels with perfect accuracy, but we can offer the same gifts to the world by trying. And, bonus, when we empathize with others, we all feel a little less alone.

Mantis' memories were wiped by the Priests of Pama to continue her adult life in Saigon. Working in a bar, she met a dashing swashbuckler named the **SWORDSMAN**, a former Avenger. Both hoped to prove themselves and join the Avengers. Interceding in a Super Villain battle, Mantis saved the team and earned spots for both her and the Swordsman. Mantis quickly became an integral

---

Super-powers: Empath
Telepath
Cosmic awareness

Skill: Gifted martial artist

Bases: Knowhere, Hala, NYC

Strange Bedfellows: Swordsman, Vision, Swordsman 2.0, the Cotati elder

Son: Sequoia the Cotati Messiah

member, often able to take down villains with her mind or with her thigh chokehold.

In fact, Mantis' strong mental discipline is the key to her physical prowess. Her mind is so clear and so connected that she can use it to control every element of her physical body. Some heroes like to punch villains now and worry about consequences later, but Mantis uses her

mind first. Studying martial arts has taught her to center herself and breathe through the stress of conflict. The calm of her quiet mind allows her to feel **EMPATHY** for her opponent, to attempt a dialogue, and to harness her emotions so that she can act logically.

Interestingly enough, Mantis is a formidable combatant because she doesn't fight angry. She enacts movements

calculated to a certain end. She isn't trying to harm anyone, but to protect those in need of her help. As a member of the Avengers, Mantis offered a rational logic to the team. Instead of heroes entering with fists blazing, Mantis would sense another creature's true desires and try to help before resorting to harmful methods. Not all who seem villainous want to watch the world burn. Using her gifts, she was sometimes able to save the day without anyone getting hurt.

Mantis fell out of love with the Swordsman and caught feels for another teammate, the sentient android **VISION**. Yes, he was a robot. Yes, that was fine with her. However, Vision was already involved with the Scarlet Witch and rebuffed Mantis' advances. While rejection can be hard, Mantis could not help but understand. If things were truly meant to work out, they would in time.

Mantis wouldn't be single for long, though she was rejected by Vision, and her former lover Swordsman died in battle. Without knowing it, Mantis was chosen by the Cotati to be raised by the Priests of Pama to become the **CELESTIAL MADONNA**, or the perfect human. Another girl named **MOONDRAGON** was also raised for this potential, and she was flawless in many ways. However, Mantis was ultimately chosen, not just because of her gifts, but because of her flaws and her true understanding of the human experience. Her loss of love for Swordsman, her desire for someone else, her mistakes, her joy, her bravery, her jealousy, her gifts, her faults all made her perfect for the role.

Vulnerability, emotion, and poor judgment may be seen as faults, but they are what make us truly human. No one is perfect. As a smart guy once said, "To err is human." While no one wants to be a human mistake factory, these blunders and their forgiveness are what bring people together. **A PERSON IS PERFECT BECAUSE THEY ARE IMPERFECT.** Humanity is a paradox—get used to it.

As the Celestial Madonna, Mantis was destined to marry the elder of the Cotati race—which just so happened to be a big telepathic tree. YES. SHE WAS PROPOSED TO BY A TREE. Well, technically a Cotati elder, which was a plant-based alien, but you get it. Listen, it's not going to get any less weird from here, so just go with it.

At first, she reacted much like we did. . . . *Say what?!* But at the Cotati's urging, she touched her head to the tree to share its telepathic link. Apparently, his bark was bigger than his bite, because she said yes! In an attempt to endear himself to her, the Cotati took on the form of her former lover, the Swordsman. She was married to him in the garden where she grew up, in a joint wedding ceremony with Scarlet Witch and Vision. You'd think it would be super awkward, marrying your tree husband in a joint ceremony with your former crush, but Mantis isn't one to get caught up in all that.

The elder Cotati revealed the secrets of the universe, allowing Mantis new cosmic awareness and the ability to travel through space in her astral form. In time, the Cotati would leave her greener in hue, but Mantis remained her impressive and powerful self. The two even conceived a child named **SEQUOIA**, who was raised by the Cotati to be the messiah of their people. For many years, Mantis traveled the universe, occasionally meeting up with the Avengers. She even briefly dabbled in a romance with Vision, when they were both single. (See, if it's meant to be, it will be.)

Mantis was eventually locked away in a Kree prison until the galaxy's most famous pain-in-the-butt hero, **STAR-LORD**, recruited her to fight some baddies at his side with his band of merry aliens, the Guardians of the Galaxy. She even used her empathic powers to help Star-Lord convince some other heroes to join his team.

Now Mantis travels the universe helping those in need and listening to their feelings. Though she has great physical power, she knows the greater power is one's mind. All life-forms need understanding and empathy, and it is the easiest thing to give.

MS. MARVEL

INHUMAN HERO. SHAPE-SHIFTER. GEEK GIRL.

KAMALA KHAN is one of the greatest heroes in the Marvel Universe, and it's not because she has a lot of hero experience. She's a devoted friend and daughter. She works hard in school. She is a level-five orc wizard in *World of Gamecraft*. She writes Super Hero fanfic. But most importantly, Kamala *cares*. She sees the world as it is and wants to make it an even better place.

Kamala is one of the few heroes who does everything in her power not to destroy a building, because she knows that it belongs to a small-business owner. She asks herself if someone really needs to be punched or if there's a less fist-forward solution at hand. Kamala is a leader—not because she forces people to obey her, but because people follow her example.

KAMALA KHAN is the Pakistani American girl next door. She loves sci-fi, video games, and geek culture, and she's a serious Super Hero fangirl. She has loving parents who try to instill in her traditional Muslim values, which means being a good person, doing your homework, steering clear of drugs and alcohol, and not spending time alone with boys.

One Friday night, Kamala asked her parents if she could attend a party with some of her friends from school, but of course with the possibility of drugs, alcohol, and definitely boys, her parents sent her to her room

instead. Feeling suffocated by all those rules, Kamala made a break for it and sneaked out.

Down at the party on the waterfront, she could see the wreck of **ATTILAN** in the harbor (which, if you remember, had fallen into the Hudson River). Kamala caught up with her friends, but between insults from her frenemies and the uncomfortable pressure to drink, she decided to bail and headed for home. Soon after she left, though, she found herself surrounded by strange mists, and something about the turn this night was taking started to feel seriously weird. A cocoon engulfed her and the mist—made of Terrigen—kickstarted a process known as "terrigenesis." Turns out that unbeknownst to her or her family, Kamala was an **INHUMAN**, and the Terrigen Mists activated her Inhuman genes, transforming her.

When Kamala awoke, she found herself with fantastic new powers. She realized she could shape-shift parts of her body (her fists, for example), making them very large and increasing her strength (a process she calls **EMBIGGENING**). She could also make herself very small, take on different appearances, and bend her body like putty.

Feeling a sense of duty to her hometown, Jersey City, she took on the moniker **MS. MARVEL** in a nod to her

---

Name: Kamala Khan

Alias: Ms. Marvel

Super-powers: Shape-shifting
Healing factor
Embiggening
Proportional strength to size

Jersey Besties: Nakia, Bruno

Skills: Straight-A student
Gifted scientist
Fanfic writer

Base: Jersey City, NJ

longtime hero, Captain Marvel, who had used the name previously. When baddies ventured across the river from New York City, Kamala was there to stop them.

The Inhuman Queen Medusa took an early interest in Kamala and her heroic tendencies. At the newly rebuilt Inhuman city of New Attilan, Medusa took Kamala under her wing for training, and even sent her teleporting canine, Lockjaw, to aid Kamala on her journey. Her actually-maybe-pretty-cute best friend, Bruno, was one of very few to know her secret and aid her as Ms. Marvel. Kamala continued to hide her heroics from her family and her friend Nakia, which slowly drove a wedge between them.

When a genius who turned himself into a birdlike figure called the Inventor began stealing teenagers to use as a renewable energy source, Kamala made it her mission to find and free the teens. Like most baddies, though, the Inventor didn't stop there. Instead, he resorted to convincing the teens that they had no worth until they volunteered to sacrifice themselves for his plans. Kamala isn't the quitting kind, so she redoubled her own efforts. She liberated the teens again and this convinced them that their lives were worth fighting for. She made it clear that kids were not responsible for adults who squandered their money, ruined the environment, and jeopardized their children's futures. Kamala showed them that kids must save the future, because **THE FUTURE BELONGS TO THEM**. Kids must find their own self-worth and never let any person—young or old—take it from them. Kids have more power than they might ever know.

Squads: All-New, All-Different Avengers; Champions

Hero Homeslices: Nova, Spider-Man, Viv, Brawn, Cyclops, Snowguard, the Wasp, Ironheart

Kamala saved the day and even got to fight alongside her hero, Captain Marvel. Captain Marvel gave Kamala a necklace that featured both their symbols—Captain Marvel's **STAR OF HALA** and Ms. Marvel's **LIGHTNING BOLT**—and provided emergency GPS should Kamala ever need to be found.

Even though she had proven herself as a Super Hero, Ms. Marvel felt disconnected from her life as Kamala Khan. Kamala returned to her family and confessed to her mother that she was Ms. Marvel. While she braced for impact, her mother revealed that she'd already known. In fact, she was very proud to call this hero, who cared for and protected people, her daughter. Kamala made amends with her friend Nakia, and even her frenemy, Zoe, who, with time, became more friend than enemy.

Her friend Bruno . . . well, Kamala finally gave Bruno time to talk, and he confessed his love for her. Though she knew it was important to figure out her feelings for him, she had other priorities. Even if her rejection meant he would move on to someone else, her life as a hero was simply more important than romantic entanglements. Her priority was saving the world, becoming the greatest Super Hero she could be, and learning things in school—and she could not let anything compromise that. Some things are just imperative, and she knew she'd have plenty of time for romance in the future when she was ready for love.

Kamala threw herself into hero life and was scouted almost immediately by Tony Stark to join his **"ALL-NEW, ALL-DIFFERENT" TEAM OF AVENGERS**. There, she met fellow young heroes Spider-Man (aka Miles Morales) and Nova (aka Sam Alexander). It wasn't all sunshine and rainbow bridges, though. Tony Stark and Captain Marvel faced off in a major fight, and Kamala's morals wouldn't allow her to continue being a part of the team. She cut ties with Captain Marvel and became her own hero. We can admire our heroes, but no one is Ms. Marvel. It's like the saying: **"DON'T SIT TOO CLOSE AT THE BALLET."** It's easy to forget the people we look up to are *people*, and that people make mistakes.

Ms. Marvel started an elite team called the **CHAMPIONS** with Miles Morales and Sam Alexander, who had also stepped away from the Avengers. They were joined by the eighth-smartest person on Earth, Amadeus Cho, who also happened to turn into a big green Hulk, later known as Brawn, as well as Viv, the synthetic sentient android daughter of Vision. In time, they would add to their ranks a time-displaced teenage Scott Summers, aka Cyclops; tiny scientist Nadia Van Dyne, aka the Wasp; Inuk teen Amka Aliyak, aka Snowguard; and Ironheart, aka Riri Williams.

CHAMPIONS

Ms. Marvel believed that though they'd once been her biggest heroes, adult Super Heroes had made a royal mess of things with their carelessness, infighting, and blatant disregard for anything beyond their missions. It was the job of the younger generation to take on saving the world in a new way—a way that used their **INTELLIGENCE AND EMPATHY** before their fists. Using Viv's search-engine-like brain, they could find people around the world who needed their help, so that they might protect them. But even more importantly, the Super Heroes began to learn about helping others the way they needed, rather than the way they *thought* people needed to be helped. Ms. Marvel reminded herokind that being a hero is less about punching bad guys and more about helping those who need it—helping can still be fun! Now, let's go **EMBIGGEN** something!

HELLCAT

CHILD STAR. HELL TOURIST. COOL CAT.

PATSY WALKER isn't your run-of-the-mill Super Hero. She wasn't born with magic powers, she didn't get doused with chemicals, and she definitely wasn't raised studying the martial arts. Patsy was a reluctant child star who made her childhood dream of becoming a Super Hero a reality as an adult. She's acquired **FANTASTIC POWERS** along her journey with her own training, hard work, and *maybe* an occasional trip through hell. After all, she did sort of marry the Son of Satan for a while. Hey, we all make some dating mistakes.

But some of the best things about Patsy are her sense of duty, her capacity for forgiveness, and her intelligence. She has used her skills as a Super Hero not just to punch, but to reform criminals and help super-powered people find legitimate career options so they don't have to turn to crime. By helping people *before* they have to turn to illicit means, Patsy is stopping the *need* for ill-gotten gains before it starts. Now that is a smart way to fight crime!

PATRICIA WALKER is a child-star-turned-Super Hero. "Patsy" grew up a classic California girl: She was a teen model and commercial actor who spent her days surfing, studying, dancing, romancing her beau Buzz Baxter, and battling her ultimate frenemy, Hedy Wolfe.

Her momager (mom + manager = momager) exploited her teen adventures as fodder for a Patsy Walker comic-book series. This boosted Patsy's fame—much to Patsy's mortification. Patsy couldn't wait to be free of her mom, and married Buzz at a young age. But she dreamed of Super Heroes and the big city. After Buzz returned from a tour of military duty, their relationship became strained and they eventually separated.

Now unattached, she finally felt free to pursue her real dreams. She hunted down **THE AVENGERS** and begged to join their ranks. Hoping to scare her out of the idea, the Avengers took her on a mission to the Brand Corporation, where her ex-husband, Buzz, now worked. The mission quickly turned upside down and revealed that her ex had become a cruel criminal. With Patsy's knowledge of her ex and resourcefulness, the team was able to finally take down the Brand Corporation. They even found a costume for Patsy that had once belonged to a hero named the Cat. The yellow catsuit gave the wearer super-strength, durability, and retractable metallic claws on her gloves and boots that are capable of slicing through most materials and enhance her climbing abilities. The team was reluctant to have her join their ranks, but she immediately put on the costume and proclaimed herself . . . **HELLCAT**!

Hey, if you want others to believe in you, you must first believe in yourself. Patsy, who had done all kinds of

---

Name: Patricia "Patsy" Walker

Alias: Hellcat

Base: Patsy Walker Temp Agency at
68 Jay Street in Brooklyn, NY

Super-powers: Increased strength and durability
Psionic enhancements
Demon sight

Skills: Martial arts
Can summon costume at will
Kitty lover

jobs, from food service to retail to television star, was ready to take on the job of being Hellcat. All heroes have to start somewhere, and this is where she began. Patsy knew she needed training and time before she could be an Avenger, but she also knew she had what it takes to make it as a hero: **COMMITMENT**. (And maybe just enough audacity and dumb luck to land herself in peril on the regular.) Like Patsy, if we hope to follow our dreams, we must go beyond fantasizing about them. We must go after what we want!

Patsy was new to the hero game, and though she did have a fabulous new outfit, she wasn't quite ready to go toe-to-toe with Super Villains. She wasn't exactly a fighter, though she was naturally athletic and her new costume enhanced those abilities. The Avengers' resident bald babe, **MOONDRAGON**, insisted that Patsy come with her to the moon Titan (where Moondragon had been educated) to be trained in psionic and martial arts. Patsy accompanied Moondragon to Titan, and even absorbed some new powers while she was there.

It's so wonderful that Patsy embraced her need for experience and education! No one knows everything, and we can all learn something from every person we meet. Furthermore, Super Heroes must work out—and work *harrrrrd*. Okay, so, maybe not Thor, because she's a god and all. But human Super Heroes have to work for it, and even our genius inventors are always trying to learn something new or perfect their next gadget. Growing and getting better is a lifelong process. There really isn't a finish line. If you work hard, you can achieve anything.

When Patsy returned to Earth, she was buff and ready to party. She joined **THE DEFENDERS** and started flirting with the Son of Satan, Daimon Hellstrom. You'd think the whole "Son of Satan" thing would be a major red flag, but sometimes it's easy to ignore obvious signs—like being an actual demon. Especially when that demon is a total hottie. When Daimon's evil was officially removed from his soul, the two decided to marry. However, her ex, Buzz (now known as the mutated villain

Mad Dog), attempted to interrupt. Despite a battle that had the ex-spouses fighting like cats and dogs, Patsy made sure Mad Dog was taken for a walk, and Daimon and Patsy were married.

The lovebirds moved to San Francisco to be paranormal investigators. However, when the evil in Daimon's soul returned in full (Hello, remember? Son of flippin' Satan?!), they separated. No one wants to couple up with an evil guy. Furthermore, Hellcat was driven mad by his malevolence. In her weakened state, she was convinced by a jerk named Deathurge to take a trip to hell. Of course, nothing goes super great in hell. She spent a lot of time battling the demon Mephisto and trying to come back to life. She was finally resurrected with the help of the Avengers. Obviously, Patsy was stoked about coming back to life, but was shaken after her stint in hell.

After making some dramatic relationship mistakes, Patsy went totally solo and built up a super-awesome support team of amazing friends. For a time, she worked as a detective for **SHE-HULK**, helping crack legal cases. However, She-Hulk had to let Patsy go when business hit a slump. This turn of events was particularly unfortunate because it meant Patsy also got kicked out of the storage closet she'd been kinda sorta secretly squatting in inside She-Hulk's office building.

Luckily, Patsy met an Inhuman named **IAN SOO** as he was committing his first crime—levitating money from an armored car. Patsy intervened and knew immediately that Ian wasn't really a bad guy—he was just really broke and very desperate. This turned on a big lightbulb for Patsy. Why not start a **SUPER-HUMAN TEMP AGENCY** to help super-powered people like Ian find jobs?! Not all super-powered people want to be Super Heroes, but they do have skills that are ideal for certain jobs. In turn, when Ian needed a roommate, Patsy moved in! Win-win!

In a bizarre twist of fate, Patsy's old **FRENEMY**, Hedy, inherited the Patsy Walker comic-book rights when Patsy's mother passed away (Patsy was in hell at the time, so she couldn't exactly execute the will). Hedy was using the old comics not just to make money off Patsy's likeness, but also to torment her! UGH! Finally, with the help of her bestie/attorney, She-Hulk, and her newfound friends, Patsy was able to prove that the contract was nonbinding, as her mother was under heavy sedation when she signed it. Patsy re-inherited the comic-book rights, which finally gave her enough money to keep that super-human temp agency open! Patsy spends her time helping super-people get jobs instead of falling into a life of crime, and, of course, kicking some evil villain butt on the side. She's one hell of a **COOL CAT**.

BFF Crew

SHE-HULK
Bestie
Legal counsel
A smash at parties

IAN SOO
Inhuman newbie
Roommate
Sassmaster

TOM HALE
Patsy's childhood pal
Ian's buff beau
Bookshop owner

HEDY WOLFE
Frenemy
Mean girl
The WORST

Evil Exes:
Buzz Baxter, aka Mad Dog
Daimon Hellstrom, aka Son of Satan

ANIMAL COMPANIONS

SUPER HEROES deserve super pets! These party animals aren't just sidekicks, they're su-purr heroes in their own right, complete with super-powers, amazing adventures, and happy tails. Even when times are ruff, we can always count on these p'awesome pals.

Dinosaurs Are a Girl's Best Friend

OLD LACE
Psychic Raptor

Gertrude Yorkes found her dino locked up for safe-keeping as a present from her time-traveling parents. Gert and her raptor buddy go by the code name Arsenic and Old Lace, based, of course, on Gert's enjoy-ment of vintage films and plays. What can I say, she has great taste! Arsenic and Old Lace share a psychic connection, so Gert can direct and control her dinosaur friend by just thinking what she wants her to do. But don't be too intimidated. Old Lace is surprisingly cuddly for a carnivorous dinosaur.

DEVIL DINOSAUR
T-Rex

Lunella Lafayette met her T-Rex partner courtesy of a portal from a prehistoric dimension. Devil Dinosaur chose Moon Girl at first sniff and they've been inseparable ever since. This twenty-foot-tall dinosaur really sticks out in a crowd, which makes it pretty hard to keep a low profile. But Devil Dinosaur is an important part of Moon Girl's battle strategy. She's the brains and he's the muscle. Well, except when the two mind-swap during the full moon and Lunella turns into a giant red lizard, and Devil Dinosaur rampages as a nine-year-old girl. Cool as it sounds, it's actually pretty inconvenient.

Unconventional House Pets

CHEWIE
Flerken

What kind of cat does Captain Marvel have? Well, a Flerken, of course! Flerkens are alien beings that look like your run-of-the-mill ginger cats, but they actually contain a pocket universe's worth of tentacles, teeth, and suckers. This really gives new meaning to the phrase "Cat got your tongue?" They are extremely dangerous, laying upward of a hundred eggs full of hungry little tentacle-mouthed kittens. However, they do make faithful pets if you can find a devoted one.

TIPPY-TOE
Squirrel

You're not really supposed to have pets in your dorm room at Empire State University, but Squirrel Girl could hardly say no to her BSFF (Best Squirrel Friend Forever), Tippy-Toe! Well, technically she lived in the tree outside of her dorm, but close enough. After college, Squirrel Girl got an apartment with her college room-mate, Nancy, so Tippy moved in with them (and Nancy's cat, Mew). Squirrel Girl and Tippy enjoy long chats (as they both speak Chitter), fighting bad guys, and of course, snacking on nuts. Tippy-Toe also effectively works as the general to her squirrel army! When Squirrel Girl needs help, Tippy and her legion of fluffy-tailed rodents are always there.

Daring Doggos

LOCKJAW
Inhuman Canine

This huge five-foot-tall, two-thousand-pound canine might look fierce, but he's all cuddles. But beware the slobber! It's not dangerous or anything, it's just wet and smelly. Lockjaw was raised by the Inhuman Royal Family and is one of the only known animals to be awarded the Inhuman transformation called Terrigenesis. With his special powers, he can play the most epic game of fetch, as he can teleport anywhere in the universe. Lockjaw has recently gone to live with the new Inhuman Ms. Marvel to aid her in her Super Hero training and to help keep her safe. Good dog.

LUCKY, AKA PIZZA DOG
Golden Retriever Mix

The Hawkeyes took in this happy-go-lucky stray from the streets of Brooklyn. Lucky only has one eye, but that just means he's always giving you a cheerful wink. He fits right in with the Hawkeyes for his love of pizza and his willingness to hang out even when things get tough. He's a big fan of snacks, long car rides with his tongue out, and, of course, ear scratches.

THE RUNAWAYS

SORCERESS. TIME TRAVELER. ALIEN. BRUISER.

THE RUNAWAYS are a team of teenagers who went on the run when they found out their parents were evil. While the team does have some boys, the ladies of the Runaways are the team's true heart and soul. **NICO MINORU** isn't just a moody goth—she comes from a family lineage that allows her to harness powerful blood magic. **GERTRUDE YORKES** might come off like a mouthy hipster, but she is the child of time travelers who gave her a pet dinosaur she shares a psychic link with. **KAROLINA DEAN**, often written off as a basic blonde, is really a super-powerful and sparkly alien. And **MOLLY HAYES** might seem like your average eleven-year-old girl who loves Super Heroes and hats, but she's actually a super-powered bruiser! These ladies have a lot to offer.

These young women have also shared the team with Chase Stein (the jock-y son of evil scientists), Alex Wilder (the super-intelligent son of mobsters), and Victor Macha (the surprisingly kind son of an evil robot). The Runaways have a habit of turning expectations on their heads because there's a lot more to these kids than meets the eye. They all have flaws, but they're all willing to put aside their needs for the greater good and for those who might need their help.

Once a year for their entire lives, Nico, Gertrude, Molly, Karolina, Chase, and Alex were forced to hang out together while their parents had meetings about their annual charity events. At one such gathering, the kids stumbled upon their parents' private discussion, but it didn't look much like event planning. Their parents were all dressed like Super Villains. Stranger still, they weren't putting their heads together over seating charts or venue rentals, but human sacrifice! Horrified and confused, the kids went on the run, vowing to stop their parents and learn how to become their own heroes.

However, the road wasn't all that easy. Molly was still in elementary school, and the rest of the team members were only teenagers. They couldn't easily get jobs without parental permission and were still learning how to take care of themselves. What was worse was that they couldn't even be seen in public: Their parents were very high profile in Los Angeles and used this to start a public manhunt for their kids.

With tensions running high, it was easy for the team to end up in screaming matches over battle plans—or really much of anything. Just like many teenagers who spent a lot of time together, love triangles formed. Team members constantly squabbled over who liked whom.

Despite all the fights and feelings, the Runaways have come together to become better people. In fact, their fights, feelings, tragedies, and ultimately their willingness to work through the hard times and support each other has cemented them together as a family. **THEY MIGHT BE CALLED RUNAWAYS, BUT THEY NEVER RUN AWAY FROM EACH OTHER.**

The Runaways: Nico Minoru
Gertrude Yorkes
Karolina Dean
Molly Hayes

Bases: Bronson Canyon Mansion
La Brea Tar Pits

NICO MINORU	GERTRUDE YORKES
Alias: Sister Grimm	**Alias:** Arsenic
Secret Weapon: Staff of One	**Secret Weapon:** Old Lace
Special Skill: Emo feels	**Special Skill:** Smack talk

If only you could make your every wish come true by saying it. Well, Nico can! Using her **STAFF OF ONE**, she can bring most any request to life—but there is a cost. She must be bleeding to summon the staff (which is a lot easier when you have your period). Her magic also requires creativity. She can never use the same wording for a spell twice, or she might elicit disastrous results, like accidentally teleporting into a far-off desert instead of "fumigating" a villain made of bees named Swarm.

As with her magic, she also struggled with saying how she felt. With so much dark magic and feelings swirling inside of herself, she wasn't always great at allowing others in. For many years, Nico felt something for Karolina, but she didn't know how to express it. Furthermore, she wasn't completely sure if her feelings were steeped in friendship or romance. Thankfully, Nico's closeness with the other Runaways over the years taught her how to open up about her emotions and **EXPRESS HER DARKNESS AND LIGHT**. After this time of growth, Nico confessed her true feelings to Karolina, and the two kissed for a second time.

Nico has learned to channel her dark feelings to better herself and to aid her friends. When she looks at them, she can always see there is light up ahead.

In an attempt to sever all ties to her former life, Gertrude Yorkes changed her name to Arsenic and dubbed her new pet dinosaur Old Lace. But having **A PET DINOSAUR THAT CAN READ HER MIND** is hardly the most interesting thing about her. She's too smart for her own good, and she'll let anyone know when they are wrong. She stands up for civil rights, doesn't tolerate **MANSPLAINING**, and is the first to jump to action when things get tough. Her passion, intelligence, and kindness draw people to her as a natural leader. It's easy to want to be Gert, because she says what's on her mind. Oh, and you know who fell in love with her? The jockiest boy in school and in the Runaways: Chase Stein. Gert exudes confidence that is irresistible. Gert doesn't have time for "conventional beauty standards." She has her own style, a body that she feels comfortable in, and a mind that she values above her external appearance. But real talk, sometimes Gert's wit and confidence get her into trouble. While saving her boyfriend and talking smack to the cruel parent that held him prisoner, she was killed. Luckily, Chase eventually found a way to time travel to save Gert and bring her to the present day. Now *that* is love.

KAROLINA DEAN	MOLLY HAYES
Alias: Lucy in the Sky	**Alias:** Princess Powerful
Secret Weapon: Rainbow solar blasts	**Secret Weapon:** Muscles
Special Skill: Sunny attitude	**Special Skill:** Naps

Karolina Dean is one of those girls that people like to pin assumptions on. Her parents are both TV actors, she is painfully pretty, she happily eats a vegan diet, and worst of all, she's *nice*. Other kids sometimes see too much "perfection" as a bad thing. They might even use it as an excuse to write someone off, because frankly, it's the easiest way to deal with jealousy. But when you take a deeper look, Karolina is far from the perfect kid everyone seems to think she is. Karolina has lived her whole life having to hold her true self back. When on the run from her parents, she discovered her truth. She had always worn a medical alert bracelet, but at the other kids' urging, she removed it. Her body filled with **SPARKLING RAINBOW ENERGY**. She could fly. She could fight. She could shoot solar blasts. Karolina was an alien called a **MAJESDANIAN** all along. Furthermore, Karolina had been knowingly hiding something else. All the scrutiny from others made it hard for her to feel that she could be open about her sexuality. After finally revealing her developing feelings for Nico, the girls kissed. Though Nico did not return her feelings at the time, Karolina was unburdened. Everyone in the group continued to love her just the same, and better yet, **KAROLINA LOVED HER TRUE SELF**.

Just because someone is little sure as heck doesn't mean they can't be a powerhouse. Molly Hayes might be pint-sized, but she's the most physically strong and durable of the group. Her powers first manifested when all of this parental drama caused an emotional response that sent Molly into **OVERDRIVE**. When she lost her cool, her powers surfaced, giving her glowing eyes and an uncanny ability to exude strength well beyond her weight class.

Like many growing kids, Molly needs massive amounts of sleep and food to recover from her exertion. Her abilities just amplify those needs, which is the downside of her particular power. But don't underestimate her—Molly is insanely tough.

However, Molly's blind trust can put her and the team in peril! From accepting a magic immortality cupcake from her school friend to being super okay with her grandma's creepy mind-reading watch-cats, Molly sometimes gives people a little too much credit. She's still a kid, and learning whom to trust can take time and experience.

Although she may not enjoy feeling like the baby of the group, the team has a responsibility to care for her. In turn, she keeps the group laughing and protects them with her great strength and **HUGE HEART**.

DORA MILAJE

ROYAL GUARD. WAKANDAN WARRIORS. ADORED ONES.

THE AFRICAN NATION of Wakanda is the most technologically advanced country in the world, and the **BLACK PANTHER** is its king. The **DORA MILAJE** (pronounced DOR-ah muh-LAH-jay) are an elite squad of fierce warriors that serve as the king's personal royal guard. Only the most talented, wellborn, and strong girls from each of the eighteen tribes of Wakanda are chosen to become part of the Dora Milaje, or **"ADORED ONES."**

They are not only trained in the deadly arts but were traditionally chosen as potential mates for the king. Though King T'Challa has put this antiquated practice to rest, he still relies on these lethal women to protect him, his sister, his mother, and his country—an amazing feat when you consider the fact that the Black Panther is already one of the most formidable heroes on Earth. It says a great deal that he relies on anyone. The Black Panther's respect for and devotion to the Dora Milaje are a testament to the strength of these incredible young women.

The Dora Milaje once held their own with only their five hundred warriors led by **CAPTAIN ANEKA** against seventy thousand highly trained military troops. That's right—these women are so dangerous they took out an entire army! But it's not just that these women are skilled or physically tough or well-armed (although they're all of that, too). What makes these women so impressive is their ability to work as a team and to lift each other up in the face of adversity.

The Dora Milaje go through intense training with Mistress Zola, the leader of the instructional facility in Upunga and a senior leader within the Dora Milaje. She offers a stern but maternal voice to the recruits as they enter the most rigorous training program of their lives to become the greatest warriors in the world. They learn a myriad of fighting styles: martial arts, traditional African hand-to-hand combat, and the use of a series of technologically enhanced weapons that can only be crafted by **WAKANDA'S BRIGHTEST.**

Base: The Golden City, Wakanda, Africa

Skills: Martial arts
Weapon mastery
Advanced technologies
Teamwork

After young women leave their families to join the Dora Milaje, they often struggle to adjust to the rigors of training or suddenly being asked to serve instead of having the run of their home. Mistress Zola sees to it that these girls become a team, a family, and work together. When a new recruit named Folami ran to Mistress Zola to tattle on the other girls in hopes of making herself look better, Mistress Zola reminded her that she must work together with the other girls and keep her eyes on her own progress first. Folami was outraged, but the Doras know that without trust in and understanding for one another, they cannot have an indestructible team. **POWER AND PROGRESS MUST FIRST COME WITH THE SHEDDING OF EGO.**

Not only must these ladies work hard to know the ways of battle, they must also work together with respect. When teammates can finally shed their judgments of one another and allow themselves to stand on equal footing with their fellow cadets, they're truly capable of becoming an incredible force.

Captain Aneka didn't just bring Wakanda one of its most impressive victories (she led those five hundred warriors, remember?). She also served the Dora Milaje as an instructor under Mistress Zola. Aneka trained new initiates in the ways of fighting and served in the personal guard for both T'Challa and his sister, **SHURI**. Seeing the crimes overlooked by the royal family in the villages of Wakanda, Aneka overstepped her boundaries and began dispensing unsanctioned vigilante justice, which included killing a chieftain who was abusing women in his village. Aneka was arrested for assassinating the chieftan, but her lover and fellow Dora Milaje, Ayo, was unwilling to watch her beloved sentenced to death. Ayo stole a prototype flying suit belonging to Wakanda's special Dora Milaje ops, the **MIDNIGHT ANGELS**, Wakanda's most lethal and skilled warriors. Ayo risked her entire life as a Dora Milaje and her personal safety to rescue Aneka. Now free, the defected Dora Milaje became vigilantes. They set their sights on protecting the people of Wakanda who were suffering in lawless territories. Internal power struggles at the palace had left many places largely unsupervised, allowing local leaders to abuse their power. Aneka and Ayo imposed swift and decisive justice against sexual predators and human traffickers, picking up where the rule of law fell short. These unsanctioned actions put them at odds with the ruler of Wakanda, but they were eventually welcomed back into the ranks of the Black Panther's unofficial guard when he required their assistance. Though their justice was brutal, these women took action to protect their communities when no one else could, which is pretty darn impressive.

> Fun Fact: Wakanda has the largest store of Vibranium in all of the world. Vibranium is an incredibly rare alien metal that absorbs vibration and is nearly indestructible. Naturally, it's an ideal material for creating weapons and advanced technologies. Due to the metal's scarcity and its high monetary worth, it's made Wakanda a target of outside foes and, on occasion, internal strife.

Two of Black Panther's closest personal guard were **NAKIA** and **OKOYE**, who traveled the world at his side. Both women risked their lives to protect their king, but Nakia's feelings for T'Challa clouded her abilities. Though T'Challa did not view these warrior women as prospective partners, he couldn't deny that he shared Nakia's feelings. When Nakia could no longer ignore her feelings for T'Challa, she was removed from the Dora Milaje. She could no longer be a part of the royal guard. Okoye continued on as T'Challa's close friend and confidante.

Ce'Athauna Asira Davin (also known as Chanté Giovanni Brown or as Queen Divine Justice when acting as a vigilante) was the princess of the White Gorilla–worshipping **JABARI** tribe. After her parents were killed in a tribal dispute, she was raised in Chicago by a Wakandan agent posing as her grandmother. When an opening became available in the Dora Milaje for the Jabari tribe, she was called back to Wakanda to serve her country.

Many intrepid women have served the Wakandan royal family, and there wouldn't even be a royal family without their protection. Their inspirational teamwork, commitment to their kingdom and communities, and incredible work ethic make these women one of the most formidable teams in the universe—without one super-power in sight. **WAKANDA FOREVER!**

AMAZING ACCESSORIES

All Wakandan citizens, including the Dora Milaje, are outfitted with Kimoyo Beads. These innocuous-seeming bracelets store an untold amount of power and information, serving as smartphones, geo trackers, full medical histories, and almost anything else you can imagine.

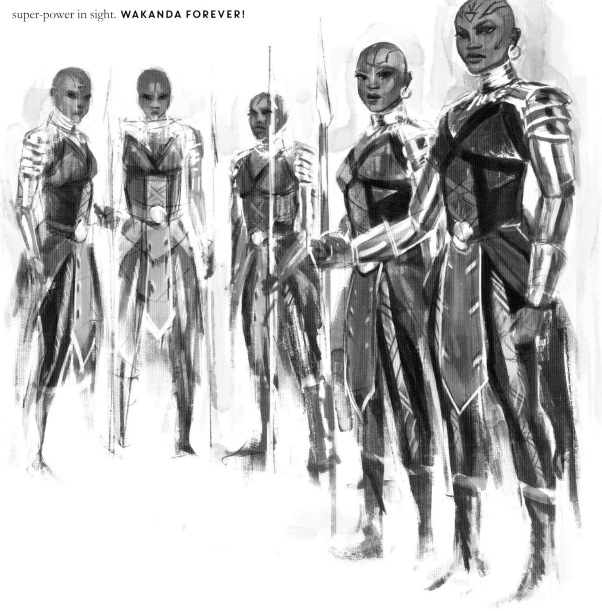

DAUGHTERS OF THE DRAGON

MISTY KNIGHT. COLLEEN WING.
NOT ACTUALLY RELATED TO DRAGONS. OR EACH OTHER.

THESE BABES are ride or die. Many Super Heroes are brought together by a mutual enemy or purpose, but these daring divas teamed up because of friendship. Through peril, near-death experiences, and even revenge, these women have stood together through it all. Their friendship is boundless and is total **#GOALS**. As both business partners and friends, they have tracked down villains, found missing persons, teamed up with Super Heroes, and have always had each other's backs. Also worth noting, these **BAD MAMMAJAMMAS** are masterful martial artists. You need someone to punch their way through a fight, '70s kung fu–style? Look no further. From Afros to women's rights, these chicks are keeping the 1970s lifestyle alive and well.

MERCEDES "MISTY" KNIGHT was raised in New York City. She was at the top of her police academy's class, and a star officer in the NYPD's 12th Precinct, where she worked as a detective.

COLLEEN WING'S mother died as a member of the Nail, a women-only strike force within an order of evil samurais called the Hand. Colleen was sent to be raised by her grandfather in Japan, where he was a member of the secret service. He taught her the ways of the samurai, passing down his thousand-year-old sword, called a katana. Colleen had recently returned to the United States to live with her father, Columbia professor Lee Wing, when she met Misty. These two ladies were pretty awesome on their own, but they'd end up being **EVEN BETTER TOGETHER**.

Misty and Colleen met under less-than-ideal circumstances. In the midst of a West Side Manhattan shootout, Misty rescued the unsuspecting Colleen from the line of fire. It was only natural the two bonded quickly, becoming best friends. I mean, a woman who can save your life is a good woman to have around, right? Misty continued to work alongside her NYPD partner, Rafael Scarfe, and Colleen continued her training in the martial arts with her new friend Iron Fist (the name sounds pretty tough, but he's actually pretty easygoing for a near-immortal martial-artist type).

While patrolling with the NYPD, Misty Knight tried to disarm a bomb that would instead literally dis-arm her. (Too soon?) Dejected and feeling directionless following the loss of her right arm, Misty decided to leave the NYPD. She felt being a civilian would be easier than resigning herself to life as a desk jockey. Misty was deeply depressed. But when life hands you lemons, and those lemons take your right hand, your friend teaches you to make sweet, sweet lemonade with your left hand! Colleen used her martial arts training to help Misty

Name: Colleen Wing

Skills: Samurai
Martial artist
Harnesses chi

Weapon of Choice: Katana

Name: Mercedes "Misty" Knight

Skills: Sharpshooter
Detective
Sass

Weapon of Choice: Bionic arm

recover her agility, improve her left-hand coordination, and most importantly, work through her depression. Martial arts teach great mental quietude, patience, and fortitude using meditation. This helped Misty to regain her confidence, not just with her new dominant hand, but in herself. With Colleen's help, Misty found new fighting skills and coordination that made her better than ever before.

Tony Stark took an interest in Misty Knight's hero tale and gifted her a **BIONIC ARM**. Misty, now ambidextrous and sporting an even more powerful right arm, became doubly lethal. She would soon be able to use her new strength to return Colleen's favor and friendship. Colleen's grandfather was murdered in Hong Kong with no one captured for the crime. Luckily, her bestie was formerly the best detective in the 12th Precinct! The two

headed to Asia to track down his killer, drug lord Emil Vachon. Together they navigated the Hong Kong underworld. Though they were forced into a number of scary situations and through a plethora of slug-fests, the ladies eventually brought the killer to justice—together.

Like all truly great unions, the whole is greater than the sum of its parts. Without their shared strength, resourcefulness, and love for each other, Misty and Colleen would not have been able to accomplish their great feats. The keys to a successful working partnership are trust, respect, and appreciation. Each is confident that their partner is skilled and has the group's best interest

Squad Goals: Heroes for Hire
- Luke Cage, aka Power Man
- Danny Rand, aka Iron Fist

Heroes for Hire 2.0
- Felicia Hardy, aka the Black Cat
- Maria Vasquez, aka Tarantula

at heart. They respect their partner's needs, boundaries, and process for getting things done. And finally, they both appreciate the contribution their companion brings to the partnership. They celebrate their victories and share their spoils. Besides, when two people share their celebrations, you get to do double the partying!

Colleen and Misty were such a terrific twosome that they started their own PI and bail-bond business—**KNIGHTWING RESTORATIONS**. Combining Misty's skills as a bionic detective and Colleen's training as a samurai, they hunted down missing persons and bad guys who skipped out on bail. Their adventures would eventually bring the ladies together with the **HEROES FOR HIRE**, run by Colleen's friend Iron Fist and his buddy with unbreakable skin, Luke Cage. Misty even caught some feels for Iron Fist. The dynamic duos would often team up and sometimes even work for each other's companies. In fact, for a while, Colleen and Misty took over the Heroes for Hire at the request of Tony Stark. The ladies employed the somewhat-reformed cat burglar the **BLACK CAT** and the Black Widow–esque **TARANTULA** to find Super Heroes trying to avoid the Super Hero Registration Act.

Though these women have taken on an endless string of street-level baddies, the two have remained dear friends through it all—with honesty, respect, and empathy. The one thing no villain can break is this duo's bond. Even when the women chose to temporarily disband Knightwing Restorations or Heroes for Hire, it never dissolved their friendship.

Misty Knight
What if we changed Knightwing to something snappier?

Colleen Wing
We've already done Heroes for Hire . . . didn't work out.

Misty Knight
How about Colsty? Mistleen? Knights of the Wing Table? Ooo, maybe we should start a restaurant called Colleen's Wings?

Colleen Wing
Are you bored? Do you want me to come over?

Misty Knight
Yes, please.

Colleen Wing
I'll bring wings.

Misty Knight
Yaaaaassss.

PEGGY CARTER & S.H.I.E.L.D.

AGENTS IN THE STREETS. LADIES WHO CAN'T BE BEAT.

S.H.I.E.L.D. cannot be spelled without the letters S, H, and E! And you can't have lady agents without **PEGGY CARTER**. Sure, S.H.I.E.L.D. technically stands for Strategic Homeland Intervention, Enforcement, and Logistics Division, but it also stands for a Whole Bunch Of Ladies Kicking Butts. Sorry, W.B.O.L.K.B. just doesn't have the same ring to it.

These fabulous women may not all have super-powers (unless you count being smart, gutsy, and strong as powers—which I do, even if the power matrix doesn't), but they certainly are heroes. These ladies are soldiers, detectives, public servants, spies, scientists, freedom fighters, and generally a special type of woman who wants to serve and protect the people around her. So let's open our super-secret S.H.I.E.L.D. file and take a look at the greatest ladies to serve.

Peggy was an all-American girl who sprang into action, joining the allies in the French resistance during WWII. It was there that she first encountered **CAPTAIN AMERICA**. They spent a few short weeks fighting side by side—and falling in love. But their romance was cut short when the war sent Cap to his next destination. Peggy felt a sense of duty to continue her mission in France, as protecting the world from Nazi domination was far more important than any romance. Peggy and Cap were separated, and an explosion affected some of her memories, but Peggy continued her career fighting for freedom as one of the first women to become an Agent of S.H.I.E.L.D.

In the early days, she worked with Nick Fury's **HOWLING COMMANDOS** and Iron Man's father, Howard Stark, all the while paving the way for future agents to change the world. In Peggy's day, agents who were women were a rarity, especially those allowed to work in the field. Though some of Peggy's memories were lost forever, some of those long-dormant memories were reawakened when Captain America found his way back into her life. Unfortunately, she was now much older than he was, thanks to Cap spending a decade or two frozen in ice. You know what they say: Love is patient, love is kind, but come on, cryogenic intervention is just unfair.

Even into her elderly years, Peggy remained a role model to the women of S.H.I.E.L.D., a lethal force against the foes of freedom and justice, and a dear friend to Captain America.

Inspo: Be like Peggy—break the glass ceiling and do things most never believed possible!

S.H.I.E.L.D. HELICARRIER
Strategic Homeland Intervention, Enforcement, and Logistics Division

NAME: Margaret "Peggy" Carter

ALIAS: Agent 13

STATUS: Covert WWII Freedom Fighter turned Agent of S.H.I.E.L.D.—RETIRED

DECLASSIFIED: Able to fight for justice backwards and in heels

S.H.I.E.L.D. HELICARRIER
Strategic Homeland Intervention, Enforcement,
and Logistics Division

NAME: Sharon Carter

ALIAS: Agent 13

STATUS: Active Executive Director of S.H.I.E.L.D.

DECLASSIFIED: Leader of the Femme Force

Hearing her aunt Peggy's stories of S.H.I.E.L.D. and WWII, **SHARON CARTER** wanted nothing more than to follow in her footsteps. After joining S.H.I.E.L.D., she was issued her aunt's former code name: **AGENT 13**. Sharon also became a covert agent and had a romance with the forever-young (and now thawed) Captain America. But let's not get caught up on how weird that family dating connection is. Instead, let's talk about how Sharon is a kick-butt agent! She was even the leader of the first **FEMME FORCE**—an elite task force of women working for S.H.I.E.L.D. Though Sharon has no super-powers, she's held her own alongside her longtime beau, Captain America, and the Avengers. She even joined the ranks of the **SECRET AVENGERS**—some of the most covert Super Heroes that have ever existed!

Inspo: Be like Sharon Carter—follow your childhood dreams!

S.H.I.E.L.D. HELICARRIER
Strategic Homeland Intervention, Enforcement,
and Logistics Division

NAME: Maria Hill

STATUS: Former Director of S.H.I.E.L.D.

CLEARANCE: Revoked

DECLASSIFIED: Tough as nails and twice as sharp

MARIA HILL is resilient, and for good reason. She survived a traumatic family life with an abusive father. She escaped by joining the Marine Corps, which was hardly an escape at all. When Maria made her way to S.H.I.E.L.D., she quickly ascended the ranks to become a top agent. Her willingness to follow even the toughest orders made her an ideal S.H.I.E.L.D. operative. She even served as the flippin' first female director of S.H.I.E.L.D.!

Outside of former Director **NICK FURY**, Hill has held the biggest role as the shadowy organization's leader. Maria gets flak for not being faithful to Fury, but she doesn't serve the man at the top. She serves S.H.I.E.L.D., whatever form it might take. Though some have questioned her methods and morals, Maria is indomitable. She's received a lot of criticism for not going easy on Super Heroes or fellow agents, but she knows it's her job to keep everyone in line, no matter how gifted they may be. She doesn't give dispensations to anyone, regardless of ability or skill level. All are equally fallible in her eyes. Even Super Heroes need someone to keep them honest and in line.

Inspo: Be like Maria Hill—be a boss!

S.H.I.E.L.D. HELICARRIER
Strategic Homeland Intervention, Enforcement,
and Logistics Division

NAME: Yoyo Rodriguez

ALIAS: Slingshot

CLEARANCE: Secret Warrior, Agent of S.H.I.E.L.D.

DECLASSIFIED: Superhuman speed

YOYO RODRIGUEZ was recruited from San Juan, Puerto Rico, as part of Nick Fury's **SECRET WARRIORS** initiative under the direction of leader Daisy Johnson, aka Quake. She is the daughter of a Super Villain named the Griffin, but was happy to be recruited by a more heroic organization. Her superhuman ability to run in any direction and then snap back to her original place earned her the code name **"SLINGSHOT."** Together with the Secret Warriors, Yoyo was instrumental in shutting down the Skrull and Hydra infiltrations of S.H.I.E.L.D. Nothing gets past someone this fast.

Inspo: Be like Yoyo Rodriguez—go your own way (and as fast as you like)!

S.H.I.E.L.D. HELICARRIER
Strategic Homeland Intervention, Enforcement,
and Logistics Division

NAME: Melinda May

ALIAS: The Cavalry

CLEARANCE: Agent of S.H.I.E.L.D.

DECLASSIFIED: Bad mammajamma

MELINDA MAY is one of S.H.I.E.L.D.'s top agents. She is a crack shot, ace pilot, and is never afraid to take the most strenuous field missions. Melinda's stoic demeanor should not be mistaken for apathy. She is deeply caring, even if she doesn't always show it. Her cool, calm, collected manner allows her to keep her wits about her when the going gets tough, because nothing is as tough as Melinda May.

Inspo: Be like Melinda May—remain cool under pressure!

S.H.I.E.L.D. HELICARRIER
Strategic Homeland Intervention, Enforcement,
and Logistics Division

NAME: Dr. Jemma Simmons

ALIAS: n/a

CLEARANCE: S.H.I.E.L.D. technician, Xenobiologist

CLASSIFIED: Secret identity as a party planner

AGENT SIMMONS is part of Coulson's elite force of S.H.I.E.L.D. operatives and has been an integral part of his team. She was recruited while still attending college, but because of her covert work, Simmons needed a secret identity. Her parents think that she is a corporate party planner! In reality, she is a top scientist and covert field agent. When Jemma was undercover at a New Jersey high school, she met a young Ms. Marvel. Not only did they team up, but Jemma also gave Ms. Marvel her card and offered a listening ear if ever the weight of keeping her secret identity was too heavy.

Inspo: Be like Jemma Simmons—offer help because even heroes need someone to talk to.

S.H.I.E.L.D. HELICARRIER
Strategic Homeland Intervention, Enforcement,
and Logistics Division

NAME: Rosalind Solomon

ALIAS: Agent E-23

CLEARANCE: Agent of S.H.I.E.L.D., currently issued use of flying car

DECLASSIFIED: Seen colluding with mysterious Thors

ROSALIND SOLOMON first encountered Thor Odinson as an Agent of S.H.I.E.L.D., and started a romantic entanglement. When the new Thor surfaced (Jane, not the son of Odin), Agent Solomon was sent in to observe and report. However, speculation was that Rosalind might BE Thor herself until it was proven otherwise. The true Thor was in fact Jane Foster, who was battling cancer in her human form. The two ladies built an important and unlikely friendship. Rosalind chose to help her sick friend instead of bringing her in for unnecessary S.H.I.E.L.D. interrogations, and has helped her on many **ASGARDIAN MISSIONS**.

Inspo: Be like Rosalind Solomon—be a loyal friend!

Though these ladies fulfill different purposes within S.H.I.E.L.D., they are all heroes. Their guts and gumption in serving and protecting are truly impressive—especially when you consider the fact that most of them don't have super-powers. These ladies have spent hours training, working to strengthen themselves mentally and physically so that they're able to handle any task. But above all, the women of S.H.I.E.L.D know what it means to be both leaders and followers. That's right, they must both lead and serve. Heck, even the director of S.H.I.E.L.D. answers to the government and the American people. These ladies know how to work hard and conquer their fears to do truly amazing things to serve others!

"Little Miss Know-It-All . . . that would be the worst thing in the whole world.

KNOWING EVERYTHING? NEVER LEARNING?

What else is there to do?!"

— LUNELLA LAFAYETTE,
MOON GIRL

IRONHEART

INVENTOR. ACCIDENTAL QUEEN. IRON WILL.

WHAT DO YOU GET when you mix the gumption and genius of Tony Stark with the heart and enthusiasm of a pint-size teen tech prodigy? Ironheart, obviously! **RIRI WILLIAMS** is a fifteen-year-old **SUPER-GENIUS** with her own Iron Man–style armor and a whole lot of tenacity. Her endless inquisitiveness and dedication have given her the skills (and the machine) needed to be a Super Hero. Though her suit does the bulk of the heavy lifting, Riri's true super-power is hard work and intellectual curiosity. No one has put Riri to the test more than herself. She was never tasked with reverse engineering an Iron Man armor—she did it to prove to herself that she could.

We can all take a page from Riri's instruction manual and make our hobbies our life's work, if we put our minds to it and follow our intellectual interests. It just takes a dash of **BRAVERY** and a whole lot of hard work. Each device and piece of Riri's mech suit requires endless iterations, but the process can be the fun part! Riri gets to discover something new every day and make it better. And trust me, something can always be better. Take it from me, a woman writing a book.

As a small child, Riri was highly intelligent. Even at a very young age, she became fascinated with building things, which evolved into a love of creating new technology. Though Riri was thrilled by her intellectual endeavors, she tended to be a solitary child. Children her age just couldn't match wits with her, but her parents wanted Riri to enjoy a normal childhood. Luckily, Riri fell into a close friendship with her neighbor Natalie. They didn't necessarily always share the same interests, but Natalie respected Riri's eccentricities and reminded her to be a kid every now and then. The girls grew very close, and Natalie was one of the few people who understood Riri.

Riri continued to stoke the fires of her creativity, eager to understand the world around her. Did I mention that **STEM** (Science, Technology, Engineering, and Math) can be very creative? STEM may have a reputation for being left-brained, but it takes wild imagination to dream up new machines, formulas, and hypotheses about the world. Riri drew her greatest STEM inspiration from the astronaut **MAE JEMISON**, who faced great challenges as the **FIRST AFRICAN AMERICAN WOMAN** to go into space, in 1992. Riri wasn't often challenged by her education, but she begged one of her teachers to create more challenges to help her be more like Jemison. That way she, too, would have something to fight for and against. Her teacher finally acquiesced and halfheartedly

Name: Riri Williams

Alias: Ironheart

Bases: Chicago, MIT Dorms
(Cambridge, Massachusetts)

Childhood Bestie: Natalie

Squad: Champions

**Mentors and Helpful
Grown-ups:** A.I. Tony Stark, Pepper Potts, Mary Jane Watson, Amanda Armstrong, Friday (Tony's A.I.), Mrs. Williams

told her she'd never be as good as Tony Stark at building tech. From that day forward, Riri set out to beat Tony Stark at his own game.

At Natalie's urging, Riri and her parents attended what was supposed to be a jovial church picnic in a Chicago park. Unfortunately, instead of summer fun, shots rang out. Riri's stepfather and Natalie were hit by a drive-by shooter in a random act of violence. Neither survived the attack. Riri's mother was devastated to lose another husband to gun violence. Riri lost not only her second father, but the only true friend she'd ever had. She dealt with her pain by throwing herself into her work like never before. She shut out the pain and kept herself busy. Very busy. Riri graduated from high school early and was accepted into the Massachusetts Institute of Technology (MIT) when she was just fifteen years old.

At MIT, Riri had all kinds of resources and tools that had never been available to her before. Using materials found on her campus, she reverse engineered Iron Man's mech suit and created her own **FLYING DEFENSIVE ARMOR**. Riri would never have to watch the people around her die in a senseless act of violence again. However, when campus security caught wind of her little project, Riri fled, going on the lam around the US.

In New Mexico, she had her first experience with stopping escaped criminals, but her armor was damaged in the fray. She wasn't quite ready for prime time. Returning to her mother's home in Chicago, she set out to repair and improve her armor as best she could. Guess who was there waiting for her? Tony flippin' Stark! I guess when you straight-up steal someone's style, they take notice pretty quickly. Awkward! Tony was truly impressed, though. With Stark's surprise blessing, Riri chose to follow in his technological footsteps as a hero. As you can imagine, her mother was less than thrilled that her only daughter was risking her life to protect the world. However, it was also painfully clear from the tragedies she had suffered that someone needed to protect people. What's more, she believed in her daughter.

Riri trained at Stark's facility, playing war games with his other armor suits and learning the finer points of being a hero. Things were going pretty great—until Tony was injured during a **SUPER HERO CIVIL WAR**. Seeing a definite need for someone to take up the mantle, Riri decided to take over for Iron Man as her alter ego, Ironheart. Though Tony was no longer around to guide her, he was kind enough to leave behind an A.I. system built from his own personality and memories. In hologram form, A.I. Tony Stark continued to assist Riri with her day-to-day problems and helped her to pilot her new Ironheart armor.

Having mentors is important for young people (and honestly, not-so-young people, too). No one knows the trials and tribulations of a field more than those who

talents and tried to recruit her. S.H.I.E.L.D. could offer Riri exciting opportunities to become a real hero. However, Riri was in no hurry to sacrifice her autonomy for a black-and-white uniform. Though Sharon was none too pleased with Riri's decision, she decided to be there when Riri needed her most—whether Riri wanted her help or not.

When it came to her daily activities, Tony's executive assistant, Mary Jane Watson, and his biological mother and CEO of Stark Industries, Amanda Armstrong, were also there to help Riri. In fact, Riri had a whole crew to assist her on her journey. Cultivating mentors might seem a strange process, but seeking out those who can help you can change your life. It certainly changed Riri's.

Riri was well on her way to becoming a full-fledged Super Hero. She even (only sort of accidentally) freed the corrupt country of Latveria. Defeating the evil ruler Lucia Von Bardas in battle, Riri became Latveria's de facto **QUEEN**! Listening to the concerns of the Latverian people, Riri saw they weren't evil—just desperately in need of assistance. Previously, the Latverian people would have had to resort to less-than-moral means to get their basic needs met. It's no wonder so many turned to lives of crime! Riri laid out a plan to get the country back on track before departing the monarchy. The job of running a country, on top of the demands of her college and Super Hero schedule, would pose real difficulties. So she set up a fair election process that restored democracy and helped the country get back on its now-democratic feet.

Riri continues sharing her iron heart with the people who need her help and the baddies who need straightening out. She often lends her muscle to **THE CHAMPIONS**, the teenage Super Hero team that solves the problems that adults can't solve or sometimes overlook. Riri is even on the short list for the **NOBEL PEACE PRIZE**! There is little Riri can't do if she puts her mind to it. Let's all strive to be as driven, passionate, and intellectually curious as Riri!

work in and around it. Fortunately, Pepper Potts, Tony's former girlfriend, past Stark Industries bigwig, and part-time hero, was also available to help Riri with the armor. They first became acquainted when the Techno Golem, Tomoe, tried to relieve both ladies of their armor using her technological manipulation. Luckily, Riri was able to outsmart Tomoe using nothing but a crappy laptop, a homemade techno virus, and a fire extinguisher. Not. Bad.

Pepper was impressed and was ready to give Riri her leave, but they had attracted more attention. The skirmish brought S.H.I.E.L.D. knocking—specifically S.H.I.E.L.D.'s executive director, **SHARON CARTER**. In the aftermath of the fight, Sharon recognized Riri's

UNSTOPPABLE WASP

RED ROOM SCIENTIST. SMALL SIZE. BIG SCIENCE.

WONDERFUL THINGS come in small packages! Just like **THE WASP**, who can shrink down to molecular levels. Though Nadia had a rough start in life, it never stopped her unbridled passion for life, science, and friendship. And what's even better? She is the namesake of the original Wasp, **JANET VAN DYNE**, who was a founding member of the Avengers and the first woman to become the chairperson of the team! Nadia is destined for greatness and has the exuberant energy and winning smile to prove it!

Nadia is the daughter of Hank Pym (aka the original **ANT-MAN** and the creator of the shrinking **PYM'S PARTICLES**) who was married before he met the original Wasp, Janet Van Dyne. Nadia's mother was Maria Trovaya, the daughter of a Hungarian geneticist. Science is in her blood! Her parents were happy—until a bunch of mysterious foreign criminals kidnapped her mother. Unbeknownst to anyone, Maria was pregnant with a daughter. Despite her dire circumstances, she named the girl Nadia, which means "hope." Maria died while imprisoned, and Nadia was raised in a secret Russian spy program. She grew up in the **RED ROOM FACILITY**, where young girls are trained to be assassins for the KGB. (Black Widow fans, you'll remember Natasha also had a "fun" stay at the Red Room!)

Fortunately, Nadia excelled at science like her parents. Recognizing her true calling, her instructors assigned her to the Red Room's "Science Class," which allowed her to focus completely on her scientific endeavors. Most girls held at the Red Room are never told who their real parents are, but Nadia was clued in on her parents' research in hopes of stoking her desire to learn. And boy, did it work. She became obsessed with her father's studies and, with hard work, she was able to duplicate Pym's Particles by using scraps of black-market research. At the Red Room, she studied alongside other gifted girls, like her friend Ying. However, if the girls formed too strong a bond, they would be separated and one of them would be replaced by another girl. Despite trying to hide their friendship, Ying was removed and sent to another class.

Name: Nadia Van Dyne

Alias: Unstoppable Wasp

Bases: Red Room Facility; Hank Pym's home in Cresskill, New Jersey; G.I.R.L. Labs

Skills: Genius-level scientist
Dancer and gymnast
Optimist
Extreme extrovert

Super-powers: Shrink to microscopic levels
Wasp blasts
Willing to share baked goods

Mentors: Janet Van Dyne
• The original Wasp
• Fashion designer
• First Avengers chairwoman

Barbara "Bobbi" Morse
• Lady adventurer
• Groundbreaking biochemist
• Hits baddies with batons

Squads: All-New, All-Different Avengers;
G.I.R.L. Champions

The Red Room was supposed to create heartless assassins and amoral scientists who would follow any and all orders without question. However, the light of Nadia's kind heart could not be extinguished. Nadia would never give up on escaping and being reunited with her family and dearest friend.

Using Pym's Particles to shrink herself, she was able to escape the Red Room and make her way to America. There, she snuck into Pym's old New Jersey home, only to learn that he had recently passed away. Though Nadia had longed for family her whole life, she picked herself up and made a new goal. Using old materials found in Pym's home, Nadia decided to continue his work, and created a Wasp costume of her own. She toiled to refine her skills and presented herself to the Avengers as **THE UNSTOPPABLE WASP**.

It took some convincing, but the Avengers finally believed Nadia was the daughter of Hank Pym, especially when she helped them correct a malfunction inside sentient robot Vision. Tony Stark's butler, Jarvis, took Nadia to meet Janet Van Dyne, who was, for all intents and purposes, her stepmother, her only surviving relative, and a fellow Wasp. As you can imagine, Jarvis was not sure how well Janet would take the news that her late husband had a secret daughter. However, Janet reacted surprisingly well because she desperately needed Nadia's help. Upon their first meeting, Janet rushed Nadia onto a helicopter headed for the White House to defuse a microverse bomb. A Super Hero's work is never done.

The mission was a success and a new friendship was born! To celebrate, Janet treated Nadia to a day of shopping, eating, and learning about her father. It was a dream! Upon their return, the Russian consul general and his men were waiting to take Nadia away. However, something about these guys seemed off. The men were members of the covert Russian team W.H.I.S.P.E.R., and they planned to return Nadia to the Red Room. The Wasps took out the bad guys, but this much was clear—if Nadia stayed in the US, she would need to sort out her citizenship as soon as possible.

Janet and Jarvis decided they would take care of Nadia, which turned out to be a full-time job. Nadia's outgoing personality had her attracting new friends wherever she went. Though Nadia's life had begun with a great deal of trauma, she never allowed that trauma to define her. She chose to let go of her past and live with hope and gratitude. Nadia embraced her new world with zeal. From donuts to car rides, there was nothing that Nadia would take for granted now that she was free from the Red Room. A second chance is hard to come by, so when it presents itself you must seize it with both hands. And eat as many baked goods as you can get said hands on.

Jarvis was responsible for watching over Nadia and making sure that she finalized her immigration paperwork, which included proving her DNA relation to Hank Pym. However, Nadia got caught up in the Super Hero stuff along the way. In fact, while battling a giant robot, Nadia met S.H.I.E.L.D. scientist, fellow adventurer, and her personal icon, **MOCKINGBIRD**. Over the moon with excitement, she gushed to Mockingbird about her scientific accomplishments. In turn, Mockingbird

G.I.R.L. Recruits

Ying
- Nadia's bestie
- Red Room lab partner
- She's the bomb

LaShayla "Shay" Smith
- Pop culture junkie
- Physics prodigy
- Style for miles

Priya Aggarwal
- Popular girl
- Secret biology genius
- Works in retail

Taina Miranda
- Genius engineer
- Lives in the Heights
- No known relation to Lin-Manuel Miranda

Ying

Priya
Aggarwal

LaShayla "Shay"
Smith

Taina
Miranda

encouraged Nadia to seek out other girls like her who were scientific geniuses. Surely with savants like herself and Lunella Lafayette coming to light, there must be many geniuses yet to be discovered. From that day on, Nadia began looking for other brilliant girls to join her new group: **GENIUS IN ACTION RESEARCH LAB**, or **G.I.R.L.**

However, the Red Room was not giving up Nadia so easily. Her dearest friend from the Science Class, Ying, was sent to bring Nadia back. However, their meeting was about to be more explosive than either wanted—because a bomb was inserted into Ying's brain. If either girl refused to comply, it would be detonated. Nadia gathered her newfound G.I.R.L. associates and they all went to work on defusing the device. Finally, using some of Vision's skin, a glove, and a whole lot of ingenuity, they were able to remove the bomb. Ying was free of the bomb and the Red Room with it! So, of course, Ying

joined the G.I.R.L. crew, never to return to the Red Room again.

Seeing what G.I.R.L. was capable of, Janet Van Dyne gave them their own area of Pym Laboratories. It seemed only fitting that Nadia take over Pym's old private floor, which was outfitted with a large laboratory and rooms for all the girls, as well as for Janet and the new G.I.R.L. Lab mentor, Mockingbird! Heck yeah! Nadia would get to learn from one of her greatest heroes. To celebrate the opening of the lab, Janet Van Dyne threw a gala for the girls, because that's what you do when you announce a fancy new lab. She took them all to get fabulous new dresses from Van Dyne's own boutique. However, Nadia overheard some sales associates talking about her father, who had a less-than-pristine past. He had had issues with violence and mental illness. Nadia was destroyed by this news. Janet had never told Nadia about her father's true nature in hopes of sparing her pain, but now that she knew there was no turning back, Janet had to help Nadia process that her father wasn't the hero of her dreams. Though he had been cruel to Janet, she had moved on and none of that was Nadia's fault. Nadia was full of love and excitement. She realized that she could both be inspired by her father's work and also be disappointed in some of his actions. His past did not change her future. Closer than ever, the two Wasps went to the party to celebrate science and girl power.

Nadia used Hank's DNA, which was found at Pym Laboratories, to prove she was indeed his daughter in order to get her American citizenship. However, Nadia had never known Hank (or her mother, for that matter), and she needed to have a last name. Janet was the closest thing to family she had ever had, so she asked if she could take the last name Van Dyne. Janet was honored and, of course, agreed! And so the Van Dyne Wasps became an **UNCONVENTIONAL LEGACY**. Plus, the Unstoppable Wasp would go on to build her own legacy alongside her fellow teenage heroes, the Champions, taking on problems big and small.

MENTORS & MATRIARCHS

HAVING A STRONG woman to look up to is a must for every Super Hero! Whether it's a mother, guardian, teacher, or friend, these experienced ladies are all an inspiration. Gray hair? Don't care! These dynamic dames are in the prime of life and they've never been better!

TRACY BURKE
Wise Friend, Wiseguy

Even a powerhouse like Captain Marvel needs someone to look up to and lean on! Not all BFFs have to be the same age, either. Tracy Burke has been a longtime friend to Carol Danvers, aka Captain Marvel, since their early days sharing an office at *Woman* magazine. Tracy doesn't take any guff, even from Carol. She's stern, but fair, and she's notorious for giving Carol the tough love she sometimes needs.

AGATHA HARKNESS
Magical Mentor

This witch has been a Super Hero governess and magic teacher for centuries! Under her tutelage, the Scarlet Witch blossomed into one of the most powerful beings in the multiverse. Even after death, Agatha, in astral form, continued training the Scarlet Witch. Just because she's dead doesn't mean she'll call in sick. Her adeptness, stern foresight, and empathetic heart have made her one of the greatest magic wielders in Marvel history.

MAUREEN GREEN
Super Mom

Get ready for the mother lode! You think your mom is embarrassingly loving? Meet Maureen Green. She's Squirrel Girl's mother and number one fan. Plus, she has the T-shirt to prove it. She makes bangin' baked goods, is a great host to Doreen and her pals, and always has an eye out for a good potential beau. Her daughter is single, after all. Know any nice boys? Maureen may not have a super-cool spy backstory, but she's just a really awesome, loving mom. What's not to like about that?!

MADAME WEB
Psychic Guide

Cassandra Webb was born blind and with a rare neurological condition that gave her psychic powers. She used her clairvoyance to aid Spider-Man in his missions, sometimes reaching out at the most opportune of moments. As a psychic, she has very good timing. She uses both her mental foresight and vast knowledge to help her young arachnid-themed heroes navigate the web of life. Though Madame Web's ethereal side may cause some people to underestimate her, she demands great respect.

MAY PARKER
Spider-Man's Aunt

May Parker is one of the most influential ladies in the Marvel Universe. Hands down. And not just because she adopted Peter Parker, who would become Spider-Man. When her husband, Ben, died at the hands of a criminal, she set out to raise Peter all on her own. Keep in mind that Peter isn't her blood relative. Yet she still put aside her life plans and raised Peter. She stood by him through all of his trials and tribulations, from studies to romance to becoming a Super Hero. Her clear moral guidance and heart made Peter the upstanding Super Hero he is today. May doesn't just matter to Peter, but touches the lives of those around her with her strong moral code, big heart, and philanthropic spirit. Now that is a real Super Hero!

RAMONDA
Wakandan Queen Mother

All hail the Queen Mother! Shuri and T'Challa learned it all from Ramonda. After the death of T'Challa's mother, N'Yami, at his birth, Ramonda raised the boy as her own. She also gave T'Challa his sister, Shuri, who was born after T'Chaka died. Ramonda brought her up to be T'Challa's equal and friend. After the death of King T'Chaka, Queen Ramonda held the country together. She remains the figurehead of the Wakandan nation. Guiding both of her children as they took over running the country, she has provided counsel, encouragement, and sometimes even hard truths. Ramonda shapes the way for Wakanda.

FREYA
Queen Goddess

The All-Mother of the Asgardian gods, Freya is more than a mother or queen—she's a mentor, too. She has raised both Thor Odinson and Loki Laufeyson as if they were her own children and ruled Asgard at Odin's side for millennia. But it's her alliance with our new Thor that's most impressive. Though Odin railed against the idea of a woman taking up his son's mantle, Freya stood up for what she knew was right, even if it meant defying her king and husband. She used her position of power to fight against the patriarchy, defending women with less influence. Now that's an action worthy of a queen!

MADRIMAR
Interdimensional Abuela

This luchador-esque lady is none other than grandmother to America Chavez. Though America spent much of her childhood lost between dimensions, her grandmother has been searching for her and guiding her. Madrimar encourages America to explore her rich ancestral past so that she never forgets her culture and familial line. She also helps America develop her super-powers and tactical skills so that she can grow as a fellow Super Hero!

MOON GIRL

SUPER-GENIUS. INVENTOR. FOURTH GRADER.

GET READY and put on your safety glasses because you're about to meet the smartest person in the Marvel Universe! Lunella might be tiny, but she's got a big brain and even bigger ideas. She happens to be only nine years old and capable of outsmarting Tony Stark, Bruce Banner, and plenty of other Marvel geniuses. Oh, and she didn't start out as the **SMARTEST PERSON ON THE PLANET** . . . but we'll get to that. From the outside, Lunella Lafayette may seem like a pretty average kid, but her disinterest in acting like a "normal" kid made her stand out—especially when she happened upon a big red dinosaur and Terrigen Mist! She also spends her time outside of school as her alter ego, **MOON GIRL**, stopping criminals, saving those who need help, and creating all kinds of inventions in her secret underground lab. There is really nothing Lunella can't do . . . except vote.

Okay, so not everything about her is strictly average. Perhaps we should start at the beginning.

On the Lower East Side of NYC, specifically Yancy Street, **LUNELLA** lives with her parents and attends school at PS 20. Lunella Lafayette was rejected from just about every gifted school there was, forcing her to continue attending PS 20, where she was . . . (how do I put this gently?) not so popular. Her classmates Zoe,

Eduardo, and the others teased her and called her names like "Moon Girl." After all, she loves space, and she does tend to space out during her more boring classes. Despite the teasing of her peers, Lunella kept herself busy with independent studies, inventions, and her reading list. Besides, Lunella had bigger worries. Like the fact that she tested positive for the **INHUMAN GENE**, and clouds of Terrigen Mists that could unlock her dormant Inhuman DNA and turn her into a freak were now floating around New York!

One day, Lunella found a **KREE OMNI-WAVE PROJECTOR** that she could use to monitor the Mists. She knew she needed to guard such a precious item. However, while she was holding the spherical object during gym class, her coach snapped it up and spun it, inadvertently opening a portal to a prehistoric alternate reality. A huge red T. rex named **DEVIL DINOSAUR** ran through, pursued by a group of monkey-like men called the Killer-Folk. (Not the way anyone wants to get out of gym class.) Devil Dinosaur snapped up Lunella, and the Killer-Folk followed them. Seeing that Devil Dinosaur meant no harm, Lunella attempted to leave him under the Brooklyn Bridge, but the Killer-Folk caught up to them. Though Devil Dinosaur helped her escape, the Killer-Folk got away and the Omni-Wave Projector was

Name: Lunella Lafayette

Alias: Moon Girl

Base: Underground Lab at PS 20, NYC

Super-powers: Smartest brain ever
Mind swap with Devil Dinosaur

Skills: Inventor
Interest in science
Great with LEGOs

lost. This was especially distressing, knowing those darn mists were out there—not to mention what those primitive primates might do with such a powerful weapon. Lunella couldn't very well ditch the big red reptile now.

Lunella and Devil Dinosaur were fast friends, but she couldn't exactly just hang with him in public. She kept him hidden in her **SECRET LAB** under PS 20. It didn't take them long to discover that they had a knack for helping people, as Lunella had the brains and Devil Dinosaur had the brawn. It seemed that things were looking up for Lunella at last! But then Brawn (or Amadeus Cho if we're going by real names) appeared, insisted a dinosaur was too big a responsibility for a nine-year-old, and took him into Avengers custody. So condescending, Brawn! Lunella couldn't accept defeat so easily and went to save her friend. Even a fancy high-security cell was no match for Lunella's wits! Lunella and Devil Dinosaur were making a break for it when they ran into the Killer-Folk. Though they defeated the hairy men and recovered the Omni-Wave Projector, Lunella didn't notice the Terrigen Mists rolling in. Lunella's body was encased in an egg-like cocoon, which Devil Dinosaur took back to the safety of her lab until she hatched. When Lunella emerged, much to her surprise, she appeared to be exactly the same. She didn't seem different at all!

All of that worrying was for nothing! Some people say, "What doesn't kill us makes us stronger," but in this case, what didn't kill Lunella made her **SMARTER**! But that wasn't all she could do. . . .

Meanwhile, far away in space, a Kree boy named Mel-Varr hoped to prove himself to his father by capturing an Inhuman. Lunella seemed like the perfect trophy. Disguised as a human named Marvin Ellis, he tried to befriend Lunella at school. However, they got into a classroom argument during a group project. At that moment, Lunella's full powers made themselves known. She appeared to go wild. Say what?! **HER BRAIN HAD ACTUALLY SWAPPED BODIES** with Devil Dinosaur! It turns out Lunella wasn't just super smart, she also

could swap minds with Devil Dinosaur anytime she got emotional or angry, or felt under duress—particularly if it was a full moon. This turned into quite a problem as Lunella attempted to fight crime or deal with high-pressure situations.

Marvin Ellis (under the alias Kid Kree) continued to try to capture Lunella by night, when her escapades as Moon Girl left her in the open. He discovered Lunella's secret lab and followed her inside. He pounced, ready to strike, but he couldn't follow through. Instead he confessed he was totally in love with her. While being rather happy not to have to battle him, Lunella could not be bothered with love. She was nine, for crying out loud! A few days later Mel-Varr's parents came to find him and bring him home. It was a relief, even if the hubbub did make Lunella lose a competition for which she built a **FULLY FUNCTIONAL CYBERNETIC TRICERATOPS** out of nothing but LEGOs.

Lunella took an intelligence aptitude test designed by Bruce Banner, which declared her to be the smartest person on Earth!

This was only the beginning for Lunella. Throughout her short life, people had rejected her from gifted programs, and being endlessly bored in class had gotten her into trouble. Finally, Lunella knew the reason! It's easy for people to be overlooked, but Lunella had finally been acknowledged for what she truly was—extraordinary!

As Lunella grew into the idea of being the smartest person around, she got to know cool teenage Super Heroes like Ms. Marvel and Ironheart, who showed her the ropes. Even geniuses don't know everything! Lunella has lots of work ahead of her. She even fashioned some Moonbots to take over for her at home and school so she could really delve into **#HEROLIFE**.

So obviously, when Moon Girl finally actually traveled around (and even visited the **ACTUAL MOON**), she had a whole new perspective on life. After seeing so many different worlds, Lunella realized she needed to return Devil Dinosaur to his home. He belonged in his own dimension, just as she belonged in hers, no matter how close they were. Devil Dinosaur tried to protest and stay with her. Though it tore at her heart, she knew he needed to go. Lunella said good-bye and left him in his home dimension. That's the hard thing about being smart—sometimes the most intelligent thing to do hurts. Especially when the other person (or in this case dinosaur) can't see that it's the right thing to do.

However, back in New York, Lunella still craved a partnership in butt-kicking. Solo Super Herodom just wasn't for her. Putting her genius mind to the test, she found that the Fantastic Four were a perfect fit! After all, they were down to two members (the ever-lovin' orange rock-covered Thing and the cool but fiery Human Torch), and they really needed a genius after losing Mister Fantastic! The Fantastic Three took to protecting New York from interplanetary menaces. However, when the chips were down, Lunella knew their team needed a fantastic fourth—not just to reinstate their catchy name, but to help them beat an enormous incoming intergalactic threat. With a little help from her handy robotic friend,

Bestie: Devil Dinosaur

Okayies: Zoe and Eduardo

Worstie: Kid Kree

Greatest Inventions: Spring-loaded skates
Punching glove
Helicopter backpack
Moon Mobile
Moonbots

she was able to retrieve Devil Dinosaur and save the Earth from being devoured!

After some time, Lunella realized that all she was looking for in a teammate was indeed Devil Dinosaur, and what the Fantastic Four really needed was the return of Mister Fantastic and the Invisible Woman. Lunella and Devil Dinosaur said their good-byes and headed off into the sunset to continue to fight crimes, save the universe, and protect her fellow kids of New York.

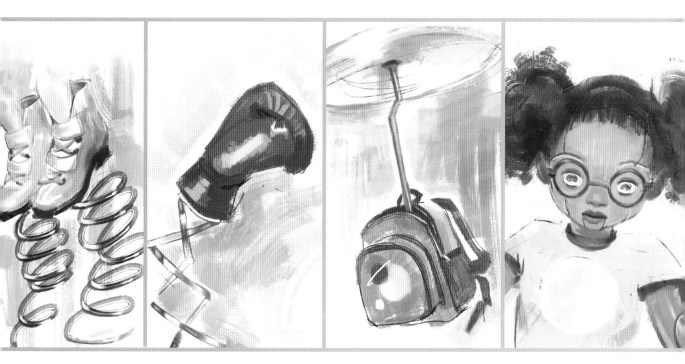

MOCKINGBIRD

MEET A SUPER HERO with a wit so snarky that they put "mocking" in her code name. She is the queen of the clapback with a punch to back it up! But **BOBBI MORSE** is far more than muscle. She joined S.H.I.E.L.D. as a lab research assistant and ended up as one of the organization's greatest agents of all time! That's right—she's a super-badass scientist! There is little Bobbi can't do if she puts her mind to it. Her examination of the Super-Soldier Serum has changed the science game, and her work in the field as a spy and Super Hero has not received *nearly* enough credit. That's the hard thing about being a spy, right?! You kind of need to keep a low profile. Despite this fact, Bobbi has had a thrilling life peppered with a whole lot of weird romances. But just because she has had a lot of boos doesn't mean she's emotionally available; she's still kind of working on that. Hey, we're all a work in progress, right?

Bobbi Morse was born and raised in San Diego, California, before attending Georgia Tech, where she worked under the tutelage of the groundbreaking scientist **DR. WILMA CALVIN**. That's right, Bobbi has been mentored by strong women from the start! Awesome! When Dr. Calvin was recruited to work on S.H.I.E.L.D.'s **"PROJECT GLADIATOR"** in the Florida Everglades,

Bobbi followed to assist her advisor. Together they hoped to re-create the Super-Soldier Serum (you know, the stuff that turns a scrawny Steve Rogers into Captain America). Bobbi Morse was inspired both by the idea and the WWI pioneering espionage vixen **MATA HARI**, so she joined S.H.I.E.L.D. spy school. She was trained in a variety of fields, from fighting techniques to subterfuge, graduating at the top of her class.

Her first mission was to travel to a secret tropical preserve in Antarctica. There she was to recruit the flowing-blond-haired, loincloth-clad hero, **KA-ZAR**. Together Bobbi and Ka-Zar scrapped with Nazis and other baddies, toiling tirelessly to protect the new incarnation of the Super-Soldier Serum that she researched with Dr. Wilma Calvin. But, hey now, Bobbi and Ka-Zar's adventures in the jungle led to a romance between the two. You could say the chemistry gave them chemistry.

Though the two managed to keep the serum out of the wrong hands, their days as a couple were numbered. When their mission together ended, so did Bobbi's tolerance for the hidden locale. She was just starting out as an agent for S.H.I.E.L.D. and wasn't about to give it all up for a guy—no matter how good he looked in fur bikini bottoms. Mockingbird had a lot of other things to learn, but she had quickly realized that her first loves

---

Name: Bobbi Morse

Aliases: Mockingbird
Agent 19
Huntress

Super-powers: Slowed aging
Increased healing
Increased physical prowess

Skills: Genius-level biochemist
Hand-to-hand combat
Weapons mastery
Avoiding talks about "feelings"

Bases: S.H.I.E.L.D. HQ, NYC, Los Angeles

were science and being an agent in the field. No matter how great the romance, there are plenty of fish with great abs left in the sea.

For Bobbi's next big mission, she was hired by Congressman Kirk to root out S.H.I.E.L.D. corruption under the code name the **HUNTRESS**. She used her new secret identity to infiltrate her own covert agency and reveal the true allegiances of several corrupt agents. In doing so, she found the real Nick Fury, who had been replaced by an **LMD**.* He filled in all the missing pieces and gave Bobbi his commendation for uncovering the secret plot. Though Bobbi did right by S.H.I.E.L.D. and her country, her secret identity as the Huntress was compromised, and she was labeled an enemy of the state. It was easier to just swap the code name and the costume.

Taking the moniker **MOCKINGBIRD** (particularly fitting because of her sass) and a new costume, she went to work for S.H.I.E.L.D. once again. However, some overzealous friendly fire left her convalescing in a hospital for six months. When she recovered, she turned down a S.H.I.E.L.D. promotion to go solo as a hero. To heck with it, right?! Sometimes a painful event can really clear a person's mind and show them what they want. In this case, she realized she did not want to kick the bucket following someone else's orders and agenda. A lot of good can come from bad things if you let it. Sure, Bobbi almost died, but the experience gave her the clarity to become the hero that she wanted to be!

Mentor: Dr. Wilma Calvin

Mentees: Wasp and the members of G.I.R.L.

Snark Level: 12 out of 12 Tony Snarks

Weapon of Choice: Battle staves

Weakness: Nice abs

Mockingbird would soon meet the Avengers' archer, **HAWKEYE** (Clint Barton). Bobbi's smart mouth wouldn't jive with Clint's less-than-trusting roguish attitude, but they were forced to work together against the attacks of the billiards-loving Odd Ball, explosive Bombshell, and sharpshooting Crossfire. Though their union was reluctant at first, the two began to work in tandem, and sparks flew. They soon discovered their skills made them an incredible team—and an incredible couple. They eloped and had a bath in a heart-shaped bathtub, because that's just what newlyweds do. It seemed Bobbi and Hawkeye were coming into their own—together. Which is the sign of a pretty good thing!

The lovebirds joined **THE AVENGERS**, but Avengers' chairman, the sentient robot Vision, had other plans for them. They were sent to open a new chapter of the Avengers on the West Coast, in Los Angeles. During the team's skirmish against the time-traveling villain Kang the Conqueror, the West Coast Avengers got stuck in the Old West, encountering a villain called the Phantom Rider. He became obsessed with Bobbi. Not like, "OMG, you're so obsessed with me." But like, "OMG. YOU'RE SO OBSESSED WITH ME."

The Phantom gave her a brainwashing potion, and Bobbi believed herself to be in love with the apparition.

* Life Model Decoy

She even began fighting by his side. She didn't know what the heck she was doing, and it certainly wasn't making her husband happy. When the potion wore off, she returned to Hawkeye's side to rid herself of the Phantom Rider. During the tussle, Bobbi let Phantom Rider fall to his death. Those final moments led to a great deal of scrutiny and strain between Mockingbird and Hawkeye. Hawkeye said he did not agree that a hero should let anyone die, even a villain. But Mockingbird was too traumatized to help the man who had brainwashed her. Phantom Rider had forced her to be his romantic partner against her will. Furthermore, Bobbi always believed that it wasn't the villain's death but her perceived infidelity that was the true cause of Hawkeye's anger. The lovebirds divorced once and for all.

Despite the couple's split, Hawkeye and Mockingbird would work together for years to come. Birds of a feather flock together—even sometimes after they get divorced. They still shared a great love and respect for each other.

Hall of Exes

Young Love: Ka-Zar
    Pros: Great survival skills, nice abs
    Cons: Antiquated ideologies, doesn't
        own pants

The One Who
Got Away: Hawkeye, aka Clint Barton
    Pros: Avenger, fun bird-themed couple
        names, nice abs
    Cons: Jealous but doesn't say he's
        jealous

On-Call Bae: Lance Hunter
    Pros: Cute British accent, doesn't mind
        if you accidentally call him
        Clint, nice abs
    Cons: Frivolous, fellow spies are hard
        to trust

Just because a couple separates doesn't necessarily mean they have to hate each other. Some incidents are just better left in the past. Bobbi and Hawkeye needed to let their relationship go, and Bobbi's newfound singleness left her open to new and different adventures.

Mockingbird still had her greatest loves: **SCIENCE AND BUTT-KICKING**. Oh, and the butt-kicking was about to get a whole lot better. She was forever changed when she was shot by agents of an opposing agency called H.A.M.M.E.R. and was treated with the Super-Soldier Serum **INFINITY FORMULA** by Nick Fury. The Infinity Formula notably gave Nick Fury his forever-young appearance and superhuman strength. Given the choice between death and life, there wasn't much of a decision to make. The formula was administered, and Bobbi woke up good as new with some additional power-ups. She had increased her physical prowess, agility, durability, and ability to heal. S.H.I.E.L.D., however, didn't really know the side effects of the formula, so lots of checkups were required, but that's the price you pay for super-powers.

Bobbi took her newfound powers back to S.H.I.E.L.D., where she met the somewhat-not-good-for-long-term-dating-but-still-totally-dreamy-and-cute-British-accent-having-fellow-agent Lance Hunter. Some relationships aren't meant to stand the test of time, especially when both people are spies with secret missions and agendas. On the upside, Lance was still totally down to take on zombies or opposing super-baddies when the chips were down—whether he and Bobbi were dating or not.

Bobbi continues to kick butts and science up by working with various Super Heroes, like Spider-Man and the Unstoppable Wasp, and with biochem research companies. In fact, she is the mentor of Genius In action Research Lab (**G.I.R.L.**), making way for more young women who, like Bobbi, want to change the world with science and heroics.

After all, every G.I.R.L. could use a good mentor.

SHURI

GET READY for a girl who is a scientific genius, a fierce warrior, and straight-up Black girl magic! **SHURI** might be the kid sister of her half brother T'Challa, but she has grown up to be one of the most important women in the long history of the African nation of Wakanda. As the daughter of King T'Chaka and Queen Ramonda, she was raised with all the charms and education befitting a princess, as well as all the physical prowess befitting **A FUTURE BLACK PANTHER**. Black Panthers, of course, being each generation's chosen protectors and rulers of Wakanda who are given special powers by the Panther God herself. Possessing a formidable mind and a warrior's body, Shuri has grown up to serve **WAKANDA** as a scientist, queen, Black Panther, and now as the **AJA-ADANNA** (a guide to Wakanda's spiritual past and keeper of Wakandan lore).

But before I give it all away, the most important thing to know about Shuri is that she is capable and adaptable, which both go a long way. When Shuri sees a task that must be done, she dives in and commits hard to becoming the very best she can be. Any task worth doing is worth doing well, whether it's scientific research, leading a country, or becoming one with **THE ANCESTRAL PLANE**.

Shuri might have been seen as a child by many in the royal palace, but she had already far exceeded the intelligence of many around her. Though her older half brother, **T'CHALLA**, was assumed to be next in line to be the Black Panther, she too wished to enter the arena and compete for the mantle in ritualistic combat. The siblings had all the same training and experience preparing to rule as both warriors and monarchs, but she was urged toward roles that were more traditionally expected for a woman in the royal family. That's patriarchy for you. She accepted T'Challa's ascent to the throne—though it pained her. Fear not, though, Shuri would soon enough find the action for which she so yearned.

Under her brother's rule, Shuri used her scientific studies to save Wakanda from Vibranium contamination caused by Super Villains that was missed by Wakanda's own chief science officer. Her impressive education led to her advancement not only in government but as headmistress of the Wakanda School for Alternative Studies, where she directed the most intelligent youths on the planet. So maybe she wasn't the queen, but her position was a huge honor and responsibility, especially in a nation built on advanced technologies created from its legendary store of the world's most valuable metal. Shuri didn't just advise the king, she was masterminding the weapons

---

Super-powers: Heightened strength
Durability
Agility
Speed
Channeling spiritual powers
Claws

Skills: Leadership
Hand-to-hand combat
Science and technology expert

Bases: Birnin Zana, aka the Golden City, Wakanda, Africa

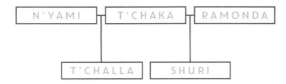

N'YAMI — T'CHAKA — RAMONDA

T'CHALLA — SHURI

and innovations of the most technically advanced country in the world as a very young woman. She also became the headmistress of the Wakandan School for Alternative Studies, directing the most intelligent youths on the planet.

Shuri finally got her chance at the crown, but not at all in the way she had hoped. T'Challa was injured in combat against an evil cabal of Super Villains—which is part of the job description, but not the way you want to go out. With T'Challa left at death's door, someone had to step up to rule Wakanda. Possessing the same aforementioned training and royal lineage, Shuri now had her opportunity to prove herself worthy. With the backing of the royal court, Shuri made the great and dangerous journey to procure the heart-shaped herb that gave the Black Panthers their increased endurance, strength, and agility. She faced a daunting mission that included fighting a pack of actual black panthers (as in *roar!*)! She conquered every challenge with panache. Let's take a moment—Shuri was the first woman known to conquer the physically grueling obstacle course that is obtaining the heart-shaped herb! This was a task taken on by only the strongest men of the nation for centuries—and this young woman **CRUSHED IT**! Okay—moving on.

Taking the herb sent her on a vision quest to be judged by the Black Panther god, **BAST**. She would either be given the great powers of her ancestors *or* be destroyed. Yikes! Tough crowd. Shuri presented herself to Bast and arrogantly proclaimed that she deserved the mantle of Black Panther for her efforts and birthright. But Bast felt that Shuri was too haughty and proud. Bast rejected her as the Black Panther, but did not demolish her.

Shuri awoke dejected and ashamed, but a pending war

waits for no woman. The cabal that had nearly killed her brother had come for the **GOLDEN CITY**, which needed its protector. Shuri had no choice but to woman up and put on the Black Panther suit to save Wakanda. Whether she had the powers of the Black Panther or not, Shuri was going to battle.

Can you even imagine how brave you must be to face such a powerful cabal alone and without super-powers?! In the act of humbling herself before her people and potentially sacrificing her life for the well-being of others, she proved to Bast that she was indeed worthy. Shuri was granted the powers of the Black Panther and became the true queen and protector of Wakanda. Oh, and she totally kicked the cabal's butts with some help from the **DORA MILAJE** and a whole lot of faith in herself.

Shuri had learned an important lesson. Yes, the Black Panther must be confident and mighty, but she must also be kind and humble. Sacrificing herself for her people proved she could be a strong leader and showed maturity. She relinquished her former sense of entitlement and earned back the trust of her people. A talented leader leads by example, with both a pragmatic mind and empathy

THE GREAT MOUND

The Great Mound is considered the Jewel of Wakanda as the the world's largest Vibranium deposit. This meteoric metal is so valuable not just because of its scarcity as an alien substance, but because of its ability to absorb vibration with its incredibly light and durable molecular structure. Weapons and suits (like the Black Panther's) are made with Vibranium, which is completely silent, nearly indestructible, and easy to wear or carry. Who wouldn't want to have a bit of Vibranium?! (Turns out a LOT of people do, and they're not all nice.)

for those around them. It can be tempting to take the lead by force, but the greatest leaders aren't the ones who shout for control—they're the ones who inspire confidence and strength in those who look to them.

As T'Challa convalesced and Wakanda recovered from the cabal's attack, Shuri served as **QUEEN** and protector of Wakanda with all the powers belonging to the Black Panther. Once he was healed, the siblings fought side by side as equals, triumphing over any who dared to invade their lands. T'Challa did not question Shuri's rule; instead he used his newfound freedom to focus on helping the Super Heroes across the world protect the planet.

When a big purple megalomaniac alien named Thanos invaded Earth, he sent a seriously nasty alien general named Proxima Midnight to lay siege to Wakanda.

As sitting protector, Shuri faced Proxima Midnight head-on. These two fierce women faced off, but Shuri alone could not stop her. Fear not, faithful reader! She did not die, but was trapped in a state of living death (kind of like being imprisoned in her own mind). In a dreamlike limbo world called **THE DJALIA**, Shuri was taught the stories of the ancestors by a spirit guide called the Griot, who presented herself in the form of Shuri's mother, Ramonda. The Griot taught her the lessons and history of her people through ancient allegories. When T'Challa was finally able to free Shuri from her dreamlike state, she retained the powers detailed in the legends she'd learned. She could now fly like birds, become tough as stone, and run faster than fire—in real life.

Shuri mastered science, diplomacy, combat, and now the spiritual realm. Is there anything this woman can't do?!

in being afraid.

Being brave isn't
the same thing
as not being scared."

— AMERICA CHAVEZ

HAWKEYE

THE BETTER ONE. YOUNG AVENGER. STRAIGHT SHOOTER.

▌BET YOU'RE THINKING . . .

Wait—isn't Hawkeye that guy named Clint Barton who shoots arrows and wears a purple mask?! Yup! *So, then, who's this chick?* Also Hawkeye! Just like Clint Barton, **KATE BISHOP** is a Super Hero who doesn't have super-powers, aims true, and holds her own! However, *unlike* Clint Barton, she comes from lots and lots of money . . . and she is probably a lot more mature than Clint, despite their age difference. But what I love most about Kate Bishop is that she took some messed-up stuff that happened to her when she was just a kid and used it as the inspiration to become a badass crime fighter. Now she's a private eye who takes down super jerks and helps out the people who need help most. Plus, she has a one-eyed dog named **LUCKY, AKA PIZZA DOG**, so you know she's doing something right.

And for real—Kate is a straight shooter (and only kind of an arrow-punner). Kate lets everyone know what's up, how she feels, what she wants, and how it's going to go down. Even with her mentor and fellow Hawkeye, Clint Barton, she seems to be just as much his teacher as he is hers. This is all largely because Kate believes in herself. She just seems to have this voice inside her saying, *Yasss, Girl, you got this.* And even when she knows she screwed up big-time, that voice seems to

say, *Okay, Girl. You messed up. Welcome to life. Everybody screws up—look at Clint Barton. Now, that's a mess. Now it's time to kick butts and make it right.* We could all use that kind of faith in ourselves.

Let's bring it back. Kate Bishop is the daughter of a very successful and crazy-rich publishing magnate named Derek Bishop and his charitable wife, Eleanor. Growing up, Kate always hoped the "too busy" businessman she called Dad would give her his approval and time. I mean, what kid doesn't want their parents' approval and time, right?! Until, of course, Kate realized that not only were her parents separating, but her father had been wheeling and dealing with Super Villains. Not long after, her mother was presumed dead. This was all awful.

Losing a parent sucks. Hard. Learning your only remaining parent might not be a great person also mega sucks. Kate was in **A REAL SUCK BUFFET**. She had a realization that many don't have until much later in life: Parents are just people. They make mistakes. Sometimes those mistakes are huge. I am going to let you in on a grown-up secret . . . most adults are just faking it and figuring it out one day at a time. The only difference is the adults have made more mistakes during their longer lifetimes, so they theoretically make fewer stupid mistakes than younger people. Theoretically. Kate found

---

Name: Kate Bishop

Alias: Hawkeye

Super-powers: Self-confidence
Having lots of money

Skills: Archery
Fencing
Hand-to-hand combat

Squad: Young Avengers 1.0

Base: Hawkeye Investigations, Venice, CA

Animal Companion: Lucky, aka Pizza Dog

Straight Shoot-o-Meter: 10 out of 10 no-bull bull's-eyes

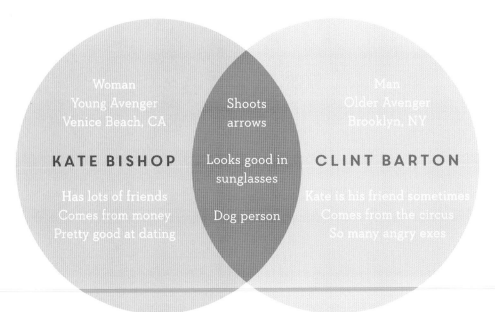

KATE BISHOP

Woman
Young Avenger
Venice Beach, CA

Has lots of friends
Comes from money
Pretty good at dating

Shoots
arrows

Looks good in
sunglasses

Dog person

CLINT BARTON

Man
Older Avenger
Brooklyn, NY

Kate is his friend sometimes
Comes from the circus
So many angry exes

out that her father was only human the hard way—by realizing he was **DEEPLY FLAWED**.

Also, the other thing about parents . . . they die. Not to super bum you out, but it's just a fact. All people die—which seems pretty obvious. We will die someday, too. Heck, even **ASGARDIANS** kick the bucket, and they are gods! But just so we aren't too bummed right now, Kate ends up okay. In fact, sometimes death is a super-great reminder to live your life to the fullest!

But bad news, Kate's life got worse before it got better. One day while walking in Central Park she was attacked. The incident left her with some serious PTSD. But rather than let the incident ruin her life, she got herself some mental health care and began to train in self-defense as well as other forms of physical combat. Endorphins from working out helped to cheer her, the therapy helped her work through her trauma, and the physical training made her ready to take on any baddie who came her way again. Bad experiences can conquer us, or we can use them as a stepping-stone to reach the next level of who we desire to be. What makes us great is what we do when facing adversity. Kate faced the suck buffet, and filled up on greatness.

Kate didn't just fall into Super Hero life, she sought it out. When armed men began taking hostages during her sister's wedding, Kate sprang into action, aiding **THE YOUNG AVENGERS**. Later, tracking down the shape-shifting Hulkling, magical Wiccan, mech-suit-wearing Iron Lad, and their patriotic leader, Patriot, Kate and new recruit Cassie Lang, aka Giant-Girl, offered their services to the team. The boys were quick to refuse, but they quickly learned they needed the girls' help, especially when Kate was able to score a bunch of Mockingbird's and Hawkeye's old battle gear from the now-defunct Avengers Mansion. When **THE AVENGERS** disbanded, the new team of all-teenage heroes stepped in to protect New York City, despite the protests of Captain America and Tony Stark.

With a big job ahead of them and no support or training, the Young Avengers managed to save the world from the time-traveling villain Kang the Conqueror, as well as stop an alien invasion. The group had more than proven themselves. Kate finally stood up to Captain America, who was continuing to pressure the team to disband. She insisted that they were heroes just like their adult counterparts, and if the original Avengers had trained her teammates in the first place instead of treating them like children, they might not be injured now. The Young Avengers were heroes, and they were never going to stop, so he'd have to accept it. (Oh yeah, Kate serves up the honesty piping hot.)

Captain America ended up giving Kate a gift, including new gear, and also giving her the name Hawkeye. After all, the archer was the only Avenger before her to stand up to him that way. Accepting her new moniker, Hawkeye continued to shoot straight and true for the Young Avengers. As the team evolved, she would meet her all-time bestie, **AMERICA CHAVEZ**, kiss a handful of cute boys, and defeat a whole bunch of evil mothers. Well, they looked like mothers, but they were actually evil interdimensional parasites.

Kate also took time to learn from her mentor Clint Barton and the two worked as Hawkeyes together—name mix-ups be darned! For a while, she even helped Clint deal with a mob infestation in his Brooklyn apartment building. But Clint's lack of honesty and general lack of emotional availability eventually led to a

falling-out between the two. Kate Bishop headed west to Venice Beach in California, letting Clint's dog, Lucky, tag along with her.

In Venice Beach, Kate was cut off from her father's riches and had to make money like a normal person, so she began taking detective cases. However, her father's old criminal dealings caught up with her. After doing business with Kate's father, a not-so-nice lady who went by Madame Masque and was known for cloning folks so she could wear them like skin suits came for Kate. And weirder yet, she seemed to find some answers about her mother's untimely death wrapped up in some long-buried family secrets. With the help of her new Venice friends, Kate finally tracked down Madame Masque. Only thing was, Madame Masque was wearing a full-on Kate Bishop clone suit! Kate faced off against Kate—battling both her inner demons and her literal self. Madame Masque was defeated, but Kate won't stop until she's solved her mother's murder. Fortunately, she has a lot of great friends to lean on. Sometimes even the other Hawkeye. **IT'S NOT HIS FAULT SHE'S COOLER, YA KNOW?**

SCARLET WITCH

CHAOS MAGIC. TWIN AVENGER. NEXUS BEING.

HOLD ON TO YOUR HAT, because things are about to get **MAGICAL**. I mean, Wanda Maximoff has "wand" in her name, so you know you're about to be spellbound. The Scarlet Witch is potentially the most powerful **SORCERER** in the Marvel Universe. Because . . . She. Can. Alter. The. Confines. Of. Reality. HELLO! This woman can turn the dang world inside out and upside down with her *mind*. Wanda also follows the beat of her own drum—she left home to become a Super Hero, married a robot, and has often created her own reality. I guess when you control chaos magic, the rules just don't apply. But spoilers: Wanda has been through some pretty messed-up stuff. Her emotions are both what make her wickedly powerful and what have sometimes led her to do some pretty impulsive and dangerous things.

WANDA MAXIMOFF and her twin brother, **PIETRO**, were raised by their Roma parents, Django and Marya Maximoff. They grew up leading nomadic lives across Europe, settling at the base of the fantastical Wundagore Mountain, until they were abducted and experimented on by the High Evolutionary. Along with being given a (secret) dark blessing by the elder god Chthon, this gave Wanda her powers of probability manipulation and chaos magic, and gave her brother super-speed. When the twins' powers manifested at puberty, the Roma people turned on them and wanted to burn them like witches. A man stepped in to save the twins, but also expected a favor in return.

Magneto, the man who rescued them, moved both Wanda and Pietro to America to work for his evil brotherhood. The twins quickly realized his intentions were possibly less than altruistic. Taking the code names **SCARLET WITCH** and **QUICKSILVER**, the twins started off a reluctant life of crime. An altercation with Super Heroes injured Quicksilver, but the heroes still came to his aid. This moment of kindness made the twins realize that they were perhaps fighting for the wrong side. Believing that they had more than paid their debt, they returned home to Europe. In general, if someone isn't trustworthy, maybe don't do their bidding.

When spots became available in the Avengers team (which were obviously advertised in the newspaper), they both felt the call to repay society. The twins became staple Avengers. Wanda was given the opportunity to refine her magic with training from the centuries-old witch Agatha Harkness, and she learned how to control the chaos magic gifted to her by Chthon, which let her harness her untold powers.

Name: Wanda Maximoff

Alias: Scarlet Witch

Super-powers: Hexes
Probability manipulation
Chaos magic

Skill: Losing it

Signature Move: Hex bolts

WHAT'S THAT HAT?!

It's not a hat, it's actually called a wimple! A wimple is a medieval form of headdress created with folded and starched cloth, usually worn as a symbol of modesty by women of many faiths—especially nuns. Wanda is not a nun . . . unless you count that she's taking nun of anyone's sass.

Being an Avenger wasn't all work. Wanda found romance with one of the most unlikely people—or, in this case, synthezoids. Though **VISION** is technically a robot, he first learned about love from observing Wanda when Quicksilver went missing. He witnessed Wanda's intense love for her brother, awakening new feelings and compassion within himself. These emotions flowered inside Vision as love for Wanda. And Wanda felt it, too.

Though many members of the group were very much team "Uh, He's A Robot," the two found a profound romantic connection. After being confronted with a near-death experience involving an interdimensional delinquent named Dormammu, they agreed to be married . . . immediately. I mean, you've got to live life while you can, right?! The two hoped despite having untraditional lives that they might follow a more traditional family path. However, Wanda and Vision were unable to have children (because uh, he's a robot). Instead she used her **CHAOS MAGIC** to will her own twin children into existence.

Which Family Is Witch

Fraternal Twin
Quicksilver

Ex-husband
Vision

Reincarnated Children
Wiccan and Speed

The Scarlet Witch has been through many adventures with the Avengers, but Wanda has not always been a joyful character. She has battled various forms of mental illness and suffering, which is particularly dangerous when you consider Wanda's hex powers manipulate probability in ways that can **SHAPE REALITY ITSELF**. Most anything Wanda can dream of, she can make happen with her mind (e.g., creating her own children). This means that her emotions and words can be incredibly dangerous. Psychology tells us humans cannot control which emotions we may be feeling. Sometimes people feel happy, sad, angry, or scared—that's just part of being a sentient being. There isn't a lot that can be done about experiencing emotions—because they are involuntary—but we can control what we do with them.

Wanda was still learning to control her emotional outbursts as well as her powers—which is an especially dangerous combo.

After Wanda and Vision joined the **WEST COAST AVENGERS**, a time-traveling baddie named Immortus had the government dismantle Vision. Gah! He was finally put back together, but he was no longer the Vision Wanda knew and loved. Their relationship deteriorated. Wanda was further distressed that the demonic Master Pandemonium stole her children's souls, effectively making them cease to exist. The Scarlet Witch began to break down. Fearing the worst, her mentor, Agatha Harkness, tried to erase the memory of the children from her mind to ease her suffering. However, when the truth came to light once again, Wanda went over the edge.

When you or I say things we may not mean out of intense feelings, it can *totally* hurt people—emotionally. When Wanda says something out of anger or fear, she can hurt people *literally*. She wanted her children back at any cost, and for the Avengers to be punished for lying to her. And that's just what she made happen: She allowed her breakdown to alter the world, invert reality, and change history. This brought many of her family's greatest wishes to fruition, including the return of her children. However, the world outside of her family was a certified dystopia. Seeing the chaos she created, she acted drastically again and overcorrected. With a few small words, she wiped the earth of super-powered mutants. Though two wrongs most certainly don't make a right, at least the heroes of Earth could begin to rebuild.

Wanda spent the years following these incidents rebuilding trust with the Avengers and aiding them in battles of **COSMIC PROPORTIONS**. Though Wanda's mistakes were dangerous, there's no denying that she is potentially the most powerful being in all of the universes. Wanda is in fact a **"NEXUS BEING,"** which can be a little confusing, but extremely cool. Let me explain. Alternate realities are dimensions where characters exist that are different but similar to ones that we know. For example, Spider-Gwen is from a reality where Peter Parker died and Gwen lived. However, there is only one Wanda in all of the realities. She is a **KEYSTONE TO THE MULTIVERSE**, which means she is basically part of the fabric of everything in all of existence. Don't get it twisted, though. Wanda has worked hard to control her emotions and her magic, and to make amends for her mistakes. We're all a work in progress.

SILK

SPIDER-BRIDE. SOFT YET DURABLE. STILL SINGLE.

SHE CRAWLS OVER WALLS, swings with the greatest of ease, and is smooth as Silk! **CINDY MOON** might have spent over a decade locked away, but she's back in the world and better than ever. Cindy is a new Super Hero and she's still learning the ropes (er, webs), but she's doing her best. She spent so many years locked up in a bunker, she's still just trying to get a handle on smartphones, Insta filters, and memes. That goes double for hero-ing. Cindy is just getting the hang of it, but that doesn't mean she isn't a straight badass. She is even more powerful than her fellow spider-bite victim **SPIDER-MAN**! Also (spoilers), she has had some rough teenage years with her family, but she's still totally dedicated to her fellow Moons. Not to mention she's kind of crushing on a ghost.

Cindy Moon grew up in a fairly conservative Korean American household with her doctor mother, Nari Moon, her teacher father, Albert Moon Sr., and her little brother, Albert Jr. Cindy and her parents clashed . . . a lot, especially Cindy and her mother. Let's just say her parents were less than impressed with Cindy's "C" average. Cindy was more interested in playing her sport of choice, hockey, and hanging out with her super-secret, super-dreamy boyfriend, **HECTOR CERVANTEZ**. Like many teens, she struggled to build her own life and identity, which was often in conflict with what her parents' dreams and expectations were for her.

One day, in hopes of seeing Hector, she planned to attend a hockey game. However, her parents weren't having it! They instead forced her to go on a school field trip to **GENERAL TECHTRONICS**. Not only was it majorly disappointing for her BF and her team, there she would encounter the same **RADIOACTIVE SPIDER** that bit Peter Parker. As you can imagine, Cindy was horrified when her body suddenly became a wall-crawling, web-shooting disaster. After having so many battles with her parents over boys and school, it felt scary to rely on them. But when the chips (or webs, in this case) were down, the Moons were there for Cindy in her hour of need. Cindy confessed her afflictions and her parents dedicated themselves to finding a cure for their daughter. Teenage years can be hard when kids struggle to earn more freedom from their parents, and that can cloud the love between them. The reality is that they often fight because parents hope to protect and improve their child.

Though things were momentarily better in her family unit, more strife was headed their way. A dimension-hopping devourer of spider-people named Morlun descended into Cindy's reality. A fellow spider-person and eccentric billionaire named Ezekiel

Name: Cindy Moon

Aliases: Silk
Silkworm
Analogue
Spider-Bride

Skills: Working on it
Great with pen and paper

Super-powers: Eidetic memory
Spider-strength and -speed
Spidey-sense
Fingertip web spinning

Sims helped Cindy escape certain death by locking her away in a bunker so Morlun couldn't find her. However, Ezekiel never returned for her. Ticktock. Days turned into weeks, weeks into years. When all was said and done she'd been locked away with no connection to the outside world for nearly fifteen years! She was now an adult, but had been utterly alone most of her life. Peter Parker (aka Spider-Man) found Cindy locked away and released her from the bunker. With Morlun dead at long last, Cindy took to the skies and swung from the tops of buildings, finally free!

Peter Parker was shocked by her speed. She was even **FASTER AND MORE AGILE** than he was. Her webs flowed naturally from her hands, including very helpful/painful barbs that attached to those she webbed up. Cindy swung excitedly all the way to her family's apartment to reunite with them. But they no longer lived there. Crestfallen, Cindy asked how long ago she could have gone free. Peter explained that Morlun had been dead for a while now—twice actually. She was furious! If he could come back once, she was sure he'd return

Friends and Enemies

Hector Cervantez
- Spectro
- High school boyfriend
- Technically dead

Felicia Hardy
- The Black Cat
- High-end thief
- Cruel boss

Lola & Rafferty
- Work at Fact Channel
- Know Silk's identity
- Very in love

to capture her. How could Peter be so stupid?! Despite her fury at Peter, something came over both of them. Something that neither of them could control. They began passionately kissing (yes, really). Something in their shared spider essence drew them magnetically together. Sheesh, get a room.

Peter helped Cindy get back on her feet, offering her a place to stay. But their intense spider attraction made them constantly want to head to smooch town whenever the other was in arm's reach. This was especially awkward because Peter was still living with his kind-of sort-of ex, Anna Maria Marconi. Worse yet, Morlun, the spider-snack connoisseur, was indeed awakened when Cindy emerged from the bunker. Deciding that Cindy was the foretold **SPIDER-BRIDE**, Morlun took it as a sign that it was time to hunt down all of the spider-people in the multiverse with his family of Inheritors and consume them all. Yuck.

With the help of Spider-Man, Cindy banded together with every Spider-Man/Woman/Animal/Robot in the multiverse to face Morlun and his evil troop. Her inexperience as a Super Hero put the team at risk more than once with her often-impulsive actions. Despite setbacks and tragic fatalities, Cindy finally learned to work together with her teammates to conquer Morlun and the Inheritors. Cindy was finally truly free.

Cindy had to figure out where to start and what she wanted her new life to be. She got herself an internship at the **FACT CHANNEL** working for the notorious blowhard and former editor-in-chief of the *Daily Bugle*, J. Jonah Jameson. J. Jonah took a shine to Cindy for being more of a pen-and-paper kind of gal. (Remember, she missed the whole information technology revolution during her time in the bunker.) The internship gave her a small income that helped her afford a new place to live with her colleague Lola and get back on her feet. It didn't last long, though—Lola's new romance with her coworker, Rafferty, soon sent Cindy back to her bunker. She wasn't up for living with another couple so soon and the bunker at least felt safe and was rent-free.

By day, Cindy worked at the Fact Channel, and tried to use the company database to track down her missing family. By night, Cindy continued moonlighting as the Super Hero **SILK**. Which quickly brought her in contact with the catty cat burglar the Black Cat, who took a dangerous interest in her. Noting Silk's Super Hero skills, the Black Cat targeted her as a potential lab rat for her planned black-market Super Villain upgrades. What's worse, the surgeon Black Cat was using to potentially slice and dice Cindy knew where the Moon family was. And just as Cindy was about to *finally* get a real lead on where to find them—the Black Cat killed him. Gah!

On the upside, J. Jonah Jameson took an interest in helping Cindy find her family, giving her a very tangible lead on her brother, Albert Jr. He was discovered in a halfway house recovering from an addiction to Goblin Serum that he had developed while being part of the gang called the Goblin Nation. Cindy was able to get Albert out and help him get clean.

She wasn't the only person who wasn't pleased with the Goblin Nation—the Black Cat didn't care for them elbowing in on her turf. Cindy began working for the Black Cat against their common rival. This gave her the opportunity to also become a double agent, informing S.H.I.E.L.D. through her contact, **MOCKINGBIRD**. Black Cat eventually discovered Silk's involvement with S.H.I.E.L.D. and nearly killed her for the betrayal. But (shock of the century) Cindy was saved by her first love, Hector Cervantez, who'd become a semi-dead Super Hero named **SPECTRO**.

Cindy was feeling very much on her own as a double agent, with no one but her ghost ex to turn to. Until one day when Lola and Rafferty walked in on Cindy putting

on her Silk costume. Despite Cindy's claims that she was just a cosplayer, the girls knew she was indeed Silk. Obviously, this was super stressful for Cindy because secret identities are supposed to be, ya know, *secret*. But the girls offered their support! In fact, they were proud of her and enveloped Cindy in a huge group hug. Finally, Cindy had someone who knew her secret, and she did not have to carry the weight of it all alone. It's important to have someone to share your secrets with, because no one can do life alone.

Things were looking up now, especially because Cindy got wind that her family might be hidden in a less-than-fun dimension called the Negative Zone. She figured what the heck, and took her BFFs along for the ride. What followed was a lot of fighting of dragon creatures and meeting up with a badass **RED KNIGHT**—who turned out to be Cindy's mom, Nari Moon! Together, the Moon women saved Cindy's father, Albert Moon Sr., who was trapped like a damsel in a tower. At last, the fam was reunited and it felt so good! High fives all around!

After a few more weird adventures with her surprisingly supportive boss, J. Jonah Jameson, Cindy decided to pack up her things and quit the news business. She had a new apartment in Washington Heights, where she now lives with her whole family on her own terms. But that doesn't mean she has severed ties with S.H.I.E.L.D. Oh no. In fact, Cindy is enrolled in S.H.I.E.L.D. Academy and preparing for her next mission! Agent Moon reporting for duty.

GWENPOOL

 Saved the BEST for last!!

ADORABLE MERCENARY. CUTUP. FOURTH-WALL BREAKER.

GWENPOOL hails from an alternate dimension called Earth-TRN565, or as Gwen calls it, "the real world." It IS the real world! Sorry, it's just going to be like this. Gwen has "medium awareness," which means she knows that I'm writing about her in a book right now. FINALLY! I have been waiting foreeeeever. Gwen, please . . . let me focus. While Gwenpool might be slightly exasperating to those around her, (Hey!) she is also one of the most fun Super Heroes to ever live. That's more like it! Because Gwen knows she is living in a Super Hero comic book, she allows herself to stand out and do things she'd never do in real life! Well, if you are going to be trapped in a comic-book world, you might as well be the star of your own story, ya know?! Totally. But that means she also has a lot to learn about being a Super Hero, because she doesn't always take the job super seriously. Valid point. BTW. Are . . . are you using Comic Sans? Yeah! It's fun and fresh and it lets you know I don't take myself too seriously! Whoa, boy. Don't hate on Comic Sans or I'll dice you. Okay, okay, no need for violence—sheesh. Can I write this section now?

Proceed.

In her home universe, Gwen Poole was a big fan of the Marvel Universe. In fact, after she left high school, Gwen just spent all of her time chilling out and reading about heroes and villains in comic books. You should read my Captain America and Spider-Man fanfic! Ahem. So when she was whisked away into the main Marvel Universe by participating in a totally shady universe-jumping sleep study, she knew what she had to do. Yeah! If you don't want to be an extra, then you need to get yourself a cool costume and maybe some knives or grenades or whatever. So that's what I did, except I didn't fill out the form very clearly for Big Ronnie's Custom Battle Spandex store, so she misread my pseudonym and thought it was Gwenpool instead of my real name, Gwen Poole. Honest mistake!

In fact, I wasn't really intended to even get my own comic book! I was first drawn into the Marvel Comics Universe by an artist named Chris Bachalo as part of a series of Gwen Stacy-themed variant covers. Ya know, after the popularity of Spider-Gwen. I was intended to be a character mash-up of Gwen Stacy and the mouthy mercenary Deadpool—and in the picture I was sitting in a pool, obviously. However, people loved me so much that they gave me my own origin story and then my own comic book! Pretty cool, right?!

Now armed with a seeming mixture of Gwen Stacy and Deadpool costume vibes, she became Gwenpool—the merc with pink tips. Since Gwen was now stuck in the

Name: Gwendolyn Poole

Alias: Gwenpool

Super-powers: Interdimensional travel
Medium awareness
Can travel through comic-book gutter space

Skills: Guns
Katanas
Not convinced this is reality

Base: NYC, Mobile

Affiliations: Agents of M.O.D.O.K.

Marvel comic-book world, she didn't think her actions could really hurt anyone, and if they did hurt someone . . . well, she didn't really care much about that, either. She first encountered Howard the Duck—who is a Duck detective also from another universe—when she was hired to steal a killer virus from a high-class cat burglar named the Black Cat for the super-evil organization Hydra, who definitely wanted to wipe out the general population. In my defense, I thought the Avengers would just handle it or something. How was I supposed to know they'd be off-planet?! Luckily, Howard was able to help her track down the killer virus and help Gwen save the world from being killed by germs. Tell them how I saved the day! . . . She drank the killer virus. I DRANK IT! Which was stupid and dangerous. And it worked!

Don't try this at home, kids.

Gwen now had a new comic-book life with no parents to support her, so she had to make some cheddah to pay those bills. It's unbelievable how expensive even a burner phone is. I mean, data, am I right?! Gwen took on a series of mercenary jobs through her tailor, Ronnie, which were executed with a hacker named Cecil. However, things got . . . weird, and Cecil was killed by the evil mechanical genius M.O.D.O.K. That's short for Mental Organism Designed Only for Killing, but M.O.D.O.K. is a handy acronym! M.O.D.O.K. forced Gwen to become one of the personal agents of his Mercenary Organization Dedicated Only to Killing (so . . . also called M.O.D.O.K.) alongside the high-jumping Batroc the Leaper, largely scientific Mega Tony, and the magic-wielding Terrible Eye.

M.O.D.O.K. eventually caught on that Gwen didn't really have all that many mercenary skills and tried to kill her! Using the new skills Gwen learned from Batroc and with some help from Cecil's ghost (oh yeah, did I mention Cecil became a ghost? Because he did), she managed to send M.O.D.O.K. to space with misfiring

Good Good Friends

Ronnie
- Costume creator
- Mission point person
- No nonsense

Cecil
- Hacker
- Gwen's Mission Control
- Ghost

Teddy Poole
- Little brother
- Natural blond
- Kind of a buzzkill

Good Bad Friends

Batroc the Leaper
- High jumper
- Gwen's mentor
- Frenchie

Sarah the Terrible Eye
- Spells
- Creepy mask
- Surprisingly good hugger

Mega Tony
- Expert chemist
- Inventor
- Big fella

Bad Bad Not-Friend M.O.D.O.K.
- Murder obsessed
- Big flying head
- Sent to space

rockets. Gwen took over M.O.D.O.K. the organization and rebranded his foot troops as the Poole Boys, complete with sassy pink matching outfits. Even though Gwen wasn't especially great at being a good guy, she learned that caring about people might actually help her become a better hero. I also got a chance to team up with Spider-Man; you know, the cool one—Miles Morales. I am a very big fan! But turns out he wasn't super into me shooting people in the face, so that kinda ended any hope of a long-term team-up. Oh, and he honestly made me kind of realize that if I didn't start to take SOME stuff seriously, I might turn into a flippin' Super Villain. That's a great thing to realize, Gwen. I'm glad you got back on track. Anyway, she even helped Mega Tony, Batroc, and Terrible Eye turn over new leaves as heroes, but it turns out Super Heroes just aren't paid very well. So yeah, they had to keep taking some mercenary-type jobs.

Ooo, tell them about some of my other stories! I've honestly had SO MANY adventures. Well, Gwen got stuck in a deadly RPG designed by the game-obsessed villain Arcade and teamed up with her namesake, Deadpool. Yeah! I also teamed up with Rocket and Groot from the Guardians of the Galaxy! And she had a run-in with her evil future self! Yeah, that was a lot to take, because even if I come off as pretty irreverent I still don't want to be EVIL, ya know? I love Super Heroes—I don't want to friggin' fight them! I want to hug them and be BFFs. So, I did the only thing I could think of to get rid of bad future me. I decided then and there to be good and fight for what's right. I would no longer be a mercenary. . . . And POOF! She disappeared! Because I control my destiny!! Take THAT, evil me!

Gwen now turned to the more altruistic path of Super Herodom, but there was something else waiting for her. That's right . . . my comic-book series was coming to an end. And UGH, it made my heart hurt so much because I KNOW I'm a comic-book character. This is my LIFE, people! But then I realized that as long as someone like you reads my comic books, I will live forever. As you read

about me in this book or when you find a trade paperback of my collected issues on a library shelf or you pick up an old issue in a comic-book store, I will live on with you. So, I never have to be sad because I will always be alive in your mind.

Oh, Gwen . . . That . . . that was surprisingly nice.

But not like when you're reading on the toilet. I have standards.

Welp. I think we're done here.

Byeeeeeeeee.

"You and me've always been like this. Always a little removed. Always . . . dreaming. Of HIGHER, FURTHER, FASTER . . . more. Always more . . .

We're gonna get where we're going, you and me . . . we'll get there . . . and we will be the stars we were always meant to be."

— HELEN COBB TO CAROL DANVERS, CAPTAIN MARVEL

POWERS OF A GIRL